The System is Unforgiving

Endorsements

"A truly ethical and moral leader, Allen is committed to providing his most valuable insights in his inspirational book in order to ease the journey for our next generation entering the work force! Allen's lessons learned are a must read for our youth and will provide a path for their success."

Dr. Michael C. Bachmann, Rear Admiral
United States Navy (retired)

"Allen is a leader in the true sense of the word. His work ethic mixed with the right amount of risk tolerance has resulted in success after success. Allen is always seeking to improve himself and those around him."

Efram R. Fuller, LCDR, Civil Engineer Corps (CEC)
United States Navy (retired)

„Allen Maxwell's unique ability to motivate diverse groups of people while identifying and overcoming issues is second to none."

Larry E. Kelley, LCDR (Surface Warfare Officer/Limited Duty Officer) United States Navy (retired)

"As a young man Allen Maxwell applied his character, intellect and leadership skills to become successful and decorated Naval Officer. Following his Navy career, Allen has applied those considerable strengths to become a successful entrepreneur. Throughout his professional life, Allen's willingness to the share his experience and insight have made him an exceptional leader whose counsel is sought by whenever important decisions are made."

John V. Garaffa, CAPT, Judge Advocate
General Corps (JAGC), United States Navy (retired)
Partner, Butler Weihmuller Katz Craig LLP

"As a man of integrity, the reader can be assured that Allen is giving sound advice that will help them achieve their goals."

Cynthia Machnov, Navy Acquisition Program Manager (GS-15), Naval Information Warfare Systems Command, Former Colleague

"Max's journey… is marked by not only professional, but also personal growth and unparalleled insight shared all along the way. I have benefited from his decisions, his discoveries, and the generous manner in which Max shares the gifts he possesses."

Clay Sellers, Commander (CDR), Surface Warfare Officer (SWO) United States Navy (Retired)

THE
SYSTEM
IS
UNFORGIVING

PLAY BY THE RULES AND WIN

ALLEN F.
MAXWELL

NEW YORK

LONDON • NASHVILLE • MELBOURNE • VANCOUVER

The System is Unforgiving

Play By the Rules and Win

© 2022 Allen F. Maxwell

Published in New York, New York, by Morgan James Publishing. Morgan James is a trademark of Morgan James, LLC. www.MorganJamesPublishing.com

A FREE ebook edition is available for you or a friend with the purchase of this print book.

CLEARLY SIGN YOUR NAME ABOVE

Instructions to claim your free ebook edition:
1. Visit MorganJamesBOGO.com
2. Sign your name CLEARLY in the space above
3. Complete the form and submit a photo of this entire page
4. You or your friend can download the ebook to your preferred device

ISBN 9781631955884 paperback
ISBN 9781631955891 ebook
Library of Congress Control Number: 2021935610

Cover Design by:
ebooklaunch.com

Interior Design by:
Chris Treccani
www.3dogcreative.net

Morgan James is a proud partner of Habitat for Humanity Peninsula and Greater Williamsburg. Partners in building since 2006.

Get involved today! Visit
MorganJamesPublishing.com/giving-back

CONTENTS

INTRODUCTION

My life, which by the American metric may be viewed as an accomplished one, has been ordered by a sequence of choices, observations, and mind-boggling events spanning decades. Born in the city of Philly, the son of a Georgia farmer, I recognized the irony embedded in rich greenery clinging to dilapidated buildings for dear life—edifices comprising an asphalt maze that had long lost its luster. By age seventeen, I negotiated my way out of this oppressive system by enlisting in the United States Navy as a junior enlisted sailor. Though challenged by a system run by certain contentious people who abused their positions of authority, I worked my way up the naval ranks to become a Chief Warrant Officer 3. While in service to the Navy, I raised my family, earned an Associate Degree in Electronics Technology, a Bachelor's in Business, and a Master's degree in Computer Information Systems, the only one of the Maxwell brothers to achieve degrees in higher education. I married a woman who would be by my side for thirty-five years and counting, and raised two highly successful daughters. Today, I own a defense contracting business that employs 70-100 personnel across nine states. I volunteer as the Chief Financial Officer for a non-profit organization that mentors students. Ensuring they graduate from college is one of its focus points. In a different focus, we mentor foster youth who are exiting the program. I am treasurer for the American Legion Riders Group, a 32nd Degree Twice Past Master Mason, and I'm an active Deacon at Mt. Erie Baptist Church in San Diego, California.

I don't regret a single one of my ups and downs or trials and tribulations. Had they not existed, I wouldn't be able to share with you my valuable observations and insights, as well as the actions I took to circumnavigate my life to a place of comfort, success, and opportunity that continues to unfold. With success comes more success, if you learn how to navigate life's systems. Don't take anything personally. This is a waste of your time.

Choose to not learn or follow certain rules, and the system is unforgiving. Decide for yourself what kind of existence you want, and what you can learn from my observations.

Life itself is a system of processes that can bring your goals into focus. Each circumstance I found myself in, ranging from personal to life-threatening, I grew a greater clarity in identifying how to enter and thrive in an environment where rules are unseen and unspoken. I took the time to identify the environment, and understand, I was not always positioned for advancement. Losing out on a promotion is not a reflection of your abilities…you are going up against an environment where you cannot thrive. Therefore, you need to work the system to get to an environment where you are appreciated and promoted. The more responsibility I took for my identification of the system I was in, the sooner I was able to get out of that system or, if I was obligated to stay for a period of time, develop the alliances to survive. In other words, I was always seeking a new level of happiness and satisfaction no matter what other people thought of my abilities.

Once you have learned to apply the observations and steps followed for one process to another, you will be able to successfully navigate any system for the life of your dreams.

My military career spanned most of my life and was where I was continuously put to task to re-align myself with the right folks politically and personally to stay afloat. I was involved in volatile situations, in varying positions of power, and working with many different kinds of people. I had to be thrown into different levels of the system to understand its use in various environments.

In my post-military life in the government sector and as a private business owner, I was exposed to a higher level of politics. Many times, I was faced with the choice to fight, give up, or be strategic. As time went on, I chose strategic. No matter what place you are in right now, even if it feels like a crazy environment you can't change, you can be strategic. You can seek proper mentorship to help you navigate to a new system. An increased acumen for awareness helped me identify various types of people, as well as the good fortune to have a mother and grandmother who saw trouble and pushed me away from it. While I grew up poor and black in a time of civil unrest, I am blessed that I found mentors throughout my life to help me course correct to the right environment that could bring me to ultimate success.

Culture prevents people from understanding the system. You must be able to say Mom or Dad could have been wrong in their teachings. They may have been limited in the areas where you now have greater exposure. You will leave people you love behind as you get to know your life goals and go for them. Through my journey I learned the world my dad grew up in is not the same word I grew up in, therefore his principles didn't apply to my life experience. Most importantly, I had to not be afraid to understand that situation and focus on my independent education in my life. All too often, people are afraid to go against their parents' principles, and this mindset holds them back from following a new path holding far more promise than the life their parents led.

I say this not to scare you, but life is an unforgiving system. The good news is when you apply rules and are observant and aware, you can circumvent any troubles that may arise and save yourself a lot of time and headache. You can focus your energies on achievements, versus frustration at why certain people or events thwart you from attaining a high level of life progression. As you read about my experiences, you can apply my evolution to whatever age or stage you are at in life. I will provide rules, through my journey, that will help you find the path to success as young as twenty.

We are built as humans to progress, expand, and evolve. In order to do so, you have to identify the environment you are in so you can navigate through it. You have to choose the right people to align with, and if you are in an environment that does not suit you, make a clear plan to get out. That system will be your demise if you know it is not serving your best interest and you stay. We have choices in life. Know who and what you want to be. If you are not clear with your direction, then you won't know how to orchestrate step one to building a life foundation. The system will swallow you up if you do not have a vigilant eye on the players.

I am assuming in reading this book that you are not a newbie to challenging systems. You are looking for solutions to success. Perhaps you are just starting out a decent career and are highly motivated but feel you feel you lack the foundation to manage all the roadblocks that may come your way. I can tell you that if you have already decided not to waste your days smoking pot and hanging out on the corner with the boys, you have already won and are on your way. I could have fallen into that life in Philly. Or not go to college and get a degree like many of the folks I graduated with from Georgia. I chose to sit in the board room and have intellectual conversations. You can't be on the corner and in the board room at the same time, you have to choose. You need to be steadfast or the system will swallow you up and you will have a hard time getting to a better place.

When you continually go after more in the system, you will receive louder feedback, and you must have courage. Through my life's travails, key observations ultimately brought me to create the Rules of the System. Apply these rules to your life, and you will thrive.

PART I

From the Streets of Philly to the Fields of Baxley

1 ~ THE RULES OF THE SYSTEM

What kept me alive and striving in my life was the identification and adherence to the fifteen Rules of the System as listed below. I built many of these rules before I was even 30 years old, so I am speaking to the young that if you play your cards right, you can set yourself up for life. If you are older, or in middle-age like me, then you get to reflect, reform and move forward with a greater wisdom than you ever knew you had before.

Take my Rules of the System as your own, or make your own set of Rules, but either way, let the life you have lived, and the systems you have navigated and are currently navigating, inform you of your compass. You cannot go wrong even if situations or people go haywire on you in your ascension in life. You will have the rules to fall back on and course correct you in all scenarios big and small.

The 15 Rules of the System

1. Seek, identify, and appreciate your mentors. They have been put in your life to push you to greatness.
2. Stay focused on the objective and continuously re-evaluate your game plan.
3. Constantly survey the environment to ensure every day you see where you are at.

4. Never become pompous or arrogant. Adversity is not the enemy; stay humble.
5. It is not important to always win; let others win.
6. Own your mistakes but don't take the fall for others.
7. Never be too demanding.
8. Be flexible to change but stand your ground ethically.
9. Stay close to your circle, which should be extremely small (1 or 2).
10. Be discerning about whom you trust with your ambitions.
11. Don't take anything personally. This is a waste of your time.
12. Don't let the haters distract you from your objectives.
13. Cut ties quickly if someone is not aligned with your vision.
14. Always have rainy-day money.
15. In marriage, effective communication is paramount.

If you apply these Rules of the System to your life, regardless of the kinds of people or the landscape, the results will be positive. My personal life experiences best illustrate my development and application of the rules, and therefore I share them wholeheartedly with you, holding back few details. Culture, race, creed, or color do not come into context when navigating the system. This is one of the first hurdles for you to overcome or it will hold you back.

Imagine what you can accomplish if you continue to apply rules to your life you have learned from each experience. That is working the system. After reading this book, I encourage you to create your own set of Rules of the System. If you do so, you can have anything you want in life. I have everything I want because I continued to learn, establish, and apply my rules. You must keep moving forward in the system of life, and not second guessing yourself along the way. You can identity the players in the schematic quickly and put into play the actions you need to take to get you through any sticky situation, or towards a greater understanding. One of the core elements of understanding and navigating life's system is the people. Identifying quickly who are the power figures, the enemies, and the allies helps you to navigate scenarios and situations quickly. Once core players have been identified, you can figure out how to be accepted into the arena where goals are shared. Identify your objectives continually while working in a particular environment. Each environment is a smaller system in the bigger system of life. Your awareness is on you. Know who you are and what you want to be. Are you looking for higher wages or being put in a trusted leadership position? The key is to understand your objective. You must begin with the end in mind. You must know the end state you are trying to achieve to recognize the key figures to focus on to get you through that particular system.

Should you choose to use my teachings and experiences as a platform to achieve success, be mindful who you share your education with. As you are implementing my knowledge to navigate conflict or adversity, you may assume someone is on your team, only to find out they are an adversary. Therefore, you must hold the Rules of the System close to the vest to deflect that person from taking you down. If you share your methods with the wrong people, they may try and use them against you.

Now that you understand life is a system, and that the application of rules will ensure more awareness of your navigation, I take you into my evolution. You can compare and contrast the players in my world to yours. While my story is a wild ride, understand what I am truly showing you are the systems. They exist in many contexts and environments. They start as early as your formative years, and mine started on the streets of Philly.

2 ~ Childhood to Adulthood

I lived in Philly and Georgia during my formative years. I had a choice to conform with the lower standards of the folks in my class or recognize I didn't belong in the place in which I was being raised. I bumped around a lot in the dark as most young people do, but in reflection I see I was more aware than I gave myself credit for. I started my learning in a system that kept cheap booze available, ensured plenty of drugs were on the street and people were killing each other claiming territories that didn't belong to them. Heck, most were renting to live in the neighborhoods. This system was every man for himself and God for us all as your only saving grace.

At eleven years old in Philly, I knew nothing better than my harsh environment. I didn't understand there was another way to live. I didn't know that inside me existed the desire for something different. Parents went to work, you went to school and every day, you got into a fight to earn respect, or some other mischief. That was the way of my world then. Life was dictated by living in the inner city. In our neighborhood, the police didn't patrol much or respond to incidents quickly. The fire department was also slow to respond. We were in an economically depressed, high crime neighborhood that was very violent. So, the city system used their resources in areas that were "deserving" (places that could thrive and make the city and system look good) as opposed to the areas that were unappreciative. I didn't know I was living in this way until I left.

Most people go through life not knowing they are a product of their environment. They assume they can't get out. So they start to integrate themselves into dangerous or faulty systems like dealing drugs or membership in a gang. You can save yourself by an awareness of how some things happening around you are not just consequences but are intentional. You are identified by others as a certain type of person and judged. If you fit the mold of the stereotype, then you are selected to do whatever the assignment for that environment. In this illustration, it may appear as happenstance, but know the system is inviting you into the circle. There is no such thing as luck, so if you are aware you want to leave an environment, preparation and opportunity should meet. The people you need to rise you up will appear and you can be guided through the process of learning how to better navigate the system you're in. In Georgia, circa 1970, the south was very racial and segregated. As a black person, you made choices, although they weren't obvious to you. There was civil unrest. You did not know the scope of the negative impact of making wrong choices. When my family moved to Georgia, I was still in junior high school. In this school there was a white principal, and there was a black principal. If you were sent to the white principal, it was because you had exceeded the black principal's authority. This meant your punishment would now be even more severe. However, the black principal wasn't there to guide you and to give you support; he was merely there to keep you in the mental system the South represents. Why do I say that? I remember a time when I was sitting in my sixth-grade science class and my teacher was talking about Louisiana State University (LSU). Here I am, a kid from Philly and I had no idea what LSU was about at this time in my life. So, I said to the science teacher, "Ma'am I thought this was a science class. What does LSU have to do with science?" And she said, "Black boy get out of my classroom and see the principal."

I was bewildered. Why do I have to go see the black principal? When I showed up at his office and told him what happened, he said to me, "Boy, I don't know why you brought your black Yankee butt down here anyway."

Now I was really confused, I didn't know why this man was identifying me as black, and I had no idea what a Yankee was. In that moment, I knew no one in this environment was really there to help me. It was all about conforming, severe punishment, and being put in my place. That was my first exposure to the difference between Philly and Georgia. I now had awareness of two systems that were systematically designed to hold black people down—to hold me down, regardless of my identification with race.

In Baxley, Georgia, the black people lived on one side of town and shopped at a certain grocery store. All the black people were only allowed to say certain things to certain people without repercussions. It wasn't like you would get publicly beaten, but you would be systematically ostracized if you didn't follow the rules.

The Police Department knew all the bad kids. So, whenever a petty crime happened, a store was broken into, or something was stolen from someone's farm, the police would go to the known bad kid's house and wait for them. In some cases, they would take them to jail and give them very harsh jail times, especially if you stole something. Funny as it was, if you committed a black-on-black murder, you received only weekend jail time. But if you stole something from one of the stores or on someone's property, you could get up with twenty or thirty years in jail. I had a cousin who stabbed an African American man multiple times and killed him.

My cousin received only weekend jail for a year, whereas the kids who lived down the road from us received five years for stealing some food. That's when I knew there was a process happening around me, and the black race was not benefiting from it.

The culmination of my observations as a young black person came down to this theory: If you had awareness of the system you were in, you could take one of two actions: Complain about unfairness and mistreatment, or learn how to be trusted among your white counterparts. What does it mean to be trusted? When asked to do a job, do it well without complaining. Maybe the first time your pay might not be what you think it should be, but instead of complaining, you accepted it and kept moving. The next time this white person calls upon you, you did not hesitate to support the request. You were considered and accepted as a member, and now you will be given a little more responsibility, maybe a little more pay and authority over other black people. For this you should be thankful and never complain.

The next go-around, this person starts to like you and tells his friend about you and what a good worker you are with completing assigned projects. Now you begin to earn a reputation as a good worker who shares the same ideas and direction the boss/employer wants to go. More responsibility is given, and more trust is shared. This action continues until you have risen to the supervisory position you desired, and your payment will be greater than expected for your actions.

While I wish the black and white divide didn't exist in my upbringing, I am grateful for the situation because it gave me various tools and rules to use with authority.

In Georgia, I was existing under conditions beyond my control but making the most of them by observing the pecking orders and social hierarchy. In your circumstances or environment, should you feel oppressed in any way, make notes of how people are rewarded and demoted. In each level of life, you will see there are different standards to the rewards system. In my teenage years, I started seeing why certain people were selected to do jobs and other were not. I learned there are perpetrators who pretended to be in the know. As an example, certain people lived above their means to look like they were a mover and shaker, but in reality, they were not. Because of my new exposure and lack of clear understand of what was happening, this puzzled me. I used to say to my older siblings I had a theory based on my observations of things happening around me. My theory was exactly my observation of people living above their means who were just showing off and couldn't afford the image they were projecting. I was right, as I learned later.

I learned early in life how you must never compromise your integrity. And if situations dictate that you do, sidestep it at all costs because if you go along to get along, the system will turn on you quickly. And you ask why? If someone in your environment knows you're willing to compromise your integrity at any cost, they will choose you and you will lose power in the system. This was not an overnight learning process; the system of life takes years of maturity, but you must always be open and willing to recognize understand and change.

Train yourself to be mindful of what you say and to whom you say it, and keep your eyes and ears open. I did this in my youth, but you can start at any age and in any system. This advice is critical because you will be given the rules for the system. You have to be open-minded and able to hear what's being said. In most cases, I believe it's imperative you to listen to what's not being said. This might sound like a lot, but it really isn't. It's just that you have to have the instinct to know what your goals are, and your goals obviously will change along the way. Your goals change because you mature, and you grow and you understand you can achieve more based on your exposure to the systems that surround you, but you have to be able to *see* them. Most people miss opportunities because of either their pride, their cultural upbringing, or their lack of understanding of life. I love talking to people who say they do not eat a certain food as an example, and they say it ignorantly because they've never been hungry enough to eat whatever they see in front of them. But this simple lesson costs people the opportunity to be involved in very successful systems because they shut it down before it even embraces them.

When I entered the Navy, events seemed to have no rhyme or reason as to how they fit into the overall picture. In this bigger system, I quickly learned I was just a number. Navy rules are a little bit different than the Marine Corps rules. The Marines are on the ground in a potential hand-to-hand situation; therefore, their rules have to be different. Their system is far more critical than the Navy's system because they are in a hand-to-hand combat situation. The Marines have little or no time for errors. Their errors are life-threatening; therefore, the rules of their system have to be strictly followed. As I learned earlier in the Navy, and as I was maturing, I had to be taught the severity of a system that was more about sustained performance than physical action. The Navy system was built on mental strength and problem-solving.

As a young man, I still was opinionated. Several trying circumstances revealed to me how playing into "the drama" does not bode well for one's best interests. Therefore, I started to practice more of an observer role. A level of equanimity infused itself into the state of mind in which I would develop rules for the system. With clarity, rather than being hot-headed, I was able to focus and store knowledge for a later date. As the years progressed and environments changed, even when faced with formidable threats, I built on my rules to navigate the system with calm observation. My practice of building equanimity continues today as we are always in the classroom of life, no matter how accomplished you look on paper.

Follow along in my journey through my childhood to adulthood and the Navy to see where in my life experiences and observations I built the rules to navigate the various systems. You can think back to what system you grew up in, and see where you may have formed ideals that no longer serve you. Then identify where you are headed now, and see if you are developing a strong foundation to go after the life of your dreams.

3 ~ Philly: Do Not Accept the Beginning as the End

As a young kid born in North Philadelphia, Pennsylvania, which was a very economically depressed area, I learned early, on my own, how to survive the streets. While my father put the food on the table, he was mainly hanging out in the streets with his friends, having girlfriends, and leaving my mother to take care of all seven children. The only time he thought parenting was necessary was to inflict corporal punishment. It didn't matter to him what the reasons were. If mom told him we needed a whooping, then I believe he took great joy in administering that butt-whooping. As the youngest of seven, I quickly learned what *not* to do from my older siblings. Watching my siblings totally miss the presence of the system was unbelievable. They blindly moved about life making the same mistakes and blaming the system for their unawareness. My brother hanging out in the streets with friends should have been aware of the birds of a feather antic, but he wasn't. The system dictates that individuals like the ones he was hanging out would get treated as problem children. It didn't matter if this was true or not; that's the way the group was going to be handled. I am grateful to have been born last in the birth order as the observer. Watching my siblings make those mistakes was a foundational life lesson that paved the way for my exploration of systems. Seeing the trouble they caused themselves and my parents, I was able to bypass that destiny.

My mom and dad were too busy working to show me the ropes of life. My dad was a trash collector for the city and my mom a housekeeper. To be more specific, it was mostly my mom trying to ensure all the bills were paid, school clothes were bought, and the house was in order. My dad was pretty useless in the equation.

The streets were tough. You had to fight to protect yourself at an early age or you would get bullied. Not like today's bullying. There was no cyberbullying on Facebook or Snapchat or any of these social media platforms. It was straightforward physical and verbal bullying in your face, and the volume and extent of it was predicated on the neighborhood you lived in.

Back then in the 1960s, the gang in Philly you belonged to was determined by the neighborhood you lived in or the street you lived on. So, for example, we lived on Willard Street, but I went to school on Tioga Avenue. Willard Street was in the 21st and Westmoreland Street gang territory and Tioga Avenue was in the 15th and Venango Street gang territory. So, each day going to school you were in the other gang's territory. You had to learn how to get along with other gang members and their environment. So, keep in mind, we're talking about *elementary school* and gangs. That's crazy, but that was the life of the inner city. Many times, I had to run home through a series of alleys to stay off the streets so I wouldn't be seen. In many cases, I built friendships with some of my classmates who lived in that area and offered a small level of protection from other gang members. It was all about recognition and acceptance.

While my children growing up were not exposed to the dangers of street life, they were still challenged by shooters and abusers in their schools. They were not molested, but they heard about it happening all around. In the 1960s, no one talked about anything like school shootings or abuse. I was just in street survival mode. Your exposure to strife and conflict at an early age was a normal happenstance. There was always the risk of getting shot, and sexual abuse was happening, but parents were less conscious about preventing it. Luckily, the level of hoodlum for my friends and I was below criminal since we were so young. There was some joy in oblivion. With no internet to distract us, we would hop on freight trains and try to break into their cargo. We had no idea if it was syrup for the Tastykake local plant or some harsh chemicals for industrial use. But our brains weren't working in logic. We were bored and we wanted to destroy. We were typical poor inner-city kids with nothing better to do.

One time we broke into a store just to see what we could get. We obtained nothing of any real value—tennis shoes and food products—but our mischievousness was indicative of the deviant mentality we had during those times. We had no moral compass or empathy for the owner of the store or community. Our parents did teach us those values, but we were hardheaded and didn't listen to them. Choosing this way of life, one would think the only obvious result could be the penal system or death. For many, it was. Death by getting caught up in gang violence or criminal situations. The possibility existed every day of being shot by the police or some innocent citizen trying to protect themselves. My mother had enough smarts to know the city would consume her boys if something didn't change. She was a country girl from Georgia. She left the farm when she was sixteen years old, so she knew if the city got to be unmanageable, she could always go back down south to the farm.

Mom left a subservient lifestyle in Georgia back in the 1940s to move north. It wasn't a bad time in Georgia, but she wanted more for herself. She was one of the few families that lived on their own farm. Living in the South is far different than living up North in the city. The country is the country and despite all of that, as an African American, you were still subservient to the masses. So, my mother left Georgia and she started out as far north as Connecticut and then migrated down through New Jersey to Philadelphia. There she met my dad. My father's family was different, also from the South, Greenville South Carolina. His family did not have the family structure, values, or assets my mother's family, so either from jealousy or envy, a lot of his extended family did not take a liking to my mother initially. They felt she was a spoiled rich woman from Georgia (rich because of the farm).

My mother was not educated through the formal education system, but she was very well educated from a life perspective. My grandmother, the matriarch, taught her well about the difference between right and wrong, good and bad. She was raised to believe in the strength of the church. So, she did her best to divert us from the street by keeping us close to God and religion. Despite all she did, we were still little deviants. My mother knew that as the city was progressing in the manner in which it was, the direction would not be conducive to her five young boys and her two daughters. The streets were violent, the school system was on strike, and a whole host of issues were happening in the city in 1970. She gave my dad an ultimatum: Basically to get his act together and move us out of this harsh environment or she would take her children down south and raise us on the farm. Mind you, none of us children were a part of this conversation or had a choice in the matter.

So, we continued living the way we did in Philly while our future was being plotted in my mother's hands. We had a typical inner-city lifestyle where we played stickball, street football, organized baseball, tops, Jacks, four-corners, and wall ball. In the summertime, we would break the fire hydrants to make the water flow freely so we could cool off and play in the water in the streets. We would continue these antics until the fire department or police would come by and turn the hydrant off. In most cases, because they knew the poor kids didn't have any other means, they would take their time to arrive. Every now and then the boys and girls club would block off the streets and have block parties. They would teach arts and crafts, looking to keep us focused on creative endeavors as opposed to mischief. Despite all the good intentions, we always figured out a way to make it into a competitive challenge. We would take simple games like tops and turn it into an extremely competitive game that would eventually turn into a fight or trash talking, or a simple snowball fight would quickly get competitive and violent with rocks in the snow.

My first system was the concrete jungle as known by all the kids living in the inner-city of Philly. Suburban living was what you saw on television, not the life we lived. There weren't very many parks or open spaces to naturally play around in. It was chaotic, but within it there was rationality amongst its players. If you grew up in these circumstances and have gone through a similar upbringing, then you understand how we had challenges at a very young age we had to survive. I don't feel sorry for myself or others who had to endure this lifestyle, especially if you were able to get out and build a life with better choices such as I am here to convey. If you are currently a young person in a tough environment, I can tell you there are better environments out there in the world you can work towards and work your way through rough stuff. Stay focused and you can change your circumstances to get out, and make a fine life for yourself..

Our next-door neighbor was a weird guy but he was my friend, and his father was weirder. They were weird because they would give their dog food and provide a spoon in his dish. Or the son would try to screw a light bulb in the dog's rear end to see if it would light up. On one particular day, the father thought his son was too soft and should fight me to prove how tough he was. I was very good with my hands in a boxing match. I learned how to fight from my older brothers. I knew I could beat his son without much effort, but he insisted that we fight. My parents were off at work and my siblings were out in the streets playing with their friends. The dad took advantage of the situation and incited this fight. I was fighting against the son and winning, so the father decided to step in. Mind you, I am eight or nine years old and he punches me in the face, knocking me out just so his son could claim the victory.

When my father learned of this event, he came home immediately and went into battle mode and wanted to fight this man for hitting his baby son. There was a lot of hubba hubba and trash talking, but this man stayed in hiding until my father cooled off. It took several months for the situation to lose its steam. This incident was just another day's event that eventually slipped away, and nothing happened. There was no conflict resolution or discussion such as we would have in a more orderly environment with kids today.

For my mother, though, none of this went unnoticed. My older siblings were having their visits to the police department and they got to see what the inside of jail was like. Not for any long length of time, just for stealing something small or acting stupid. They had to do the overnight stay. But again, that was typical. Fortunately for me and my sister, who was a year older than me, as the two youngest of the family we never had to experience jail.

We were smart enough to see what the older siblings were doing and not repeat their actions. We dodged the penal system and for that I am grateful. Having a great impact, I would repeat and hone this observational behavior in my young adult life. Each observation made from a keen standpoint of understanding that life is a continual system and would lead me to the next series of opportunities and blessings to not be taken lightly.

In the summer of 1970, my mother finally enacted the ultimatum she had given my dad. The school system was having problems, the violence in the streets was getting worse. My dad was not displaying any desire or effort to help make change for his kids. She kept her promise and loaded all seven of us up on an Amtrak train. Off we went to a little town called Baxley, Georgia. I am forever grateful to my mother for this, because I don't know what would have happened to me on the streets of Philly had I stayed.

4 ~ THE TOBACCO FIELDS OF BAXLEY: THE FIELDS WERE NO JOKE

Oh my heavens, talk about culture shock. In the earlier years when we would go down South for summer vacations, my grandmother kept us protected on the farm from the reality of the town. She did not let us interact with the locals too much, only with relatives. So, we had no idea what the real southern people were all about. During that time, much of the South was re-litigating the Civil War. It was violent and emotional, with Georgia's largest riot taking place in Augusta the year we arrived. My name went from Allen to boy to the n-word. As a young eleven-year-old kid from the city, I had no idea about racists. I didn't understand racism, and especially not the mentality of the locals. Not being exposed or having a whole lot of understanding of what truly happened in the Civil War, I had no idea what a Yankee was, but from 1970 through 1977 the people still called the Northerners Yankees. What I did know was I did not like it, nor was I going to subscribe to that way of life. This survival was visceral and cutting to the core.

So now my individuation as a boy is coming into form and I'm somewhat analytical. I was not like my other brothers and sisters. They quickly adjusted to the environment. I did not, but I managed. I took the time to try to learn what it was all about and what life was going to be like in the Deep South. This system is very big. Consider this: In America, the country knows right and wrong, good and bad, yet in the south, the rules every other American had to abide by didn't apply. These small country towns had family and friends in all the key places. The judge, the lawyers, the store owners, the schoolteachers, the baker, and heck even the preachers in the churches. The south was not going to change. If you go against the system, you will get bad advice from the lawyer, no opportunities for a loan at the bank, and the teacher ensured your child would not be placed in a position of success. These are just some examples of how the system worked silently and quietly with no exchange of words. A form of glass walls and ceilings. Never become pompous or arrogant. Adversity is not the enemy; stay humble.

I knew early on I had to have an exit strategy. I didn't know how I was going to get out of that environment; I just knew I wanted out. While the streets of Philly had been a contentious system, I navigated it with sheer courage and force. This system did not feel as easily surmountable. Everything was slow, no one was in a hurry to do anything. They even talked slow and used improper English. It was like going back in time thirty or forty years. Imagine living in a fast-paced inner city and then going through a time warp, landing back in time. That is what it was like moving from Philly to Georgia in 1970.

My mother initially moved us into my grandmother's house. My grandmother had a three-bedroom shotgun home. When you opened the front and back door, you could see completely through the house. The bedrooms were off to the left side of the house and the living room and dining room were combined. The last room on the right was the kitchen. In 1970, there was no indoor plumbing, so we used an out-house and large tin-tubs to bathe in.

I decided if I was here in the South, I might as well learn what it was like to be a country boy. So, I went into the fields to experience all the logistical aspects of fieldwork. I learned how to crop tobacco, pick peas, beans, cucumbers, watermelons, and a whole host of other farm items. I learned how to ride horses, and the techniques of fishing. I learned about what it's like to "live off the grid" as we call it today. We were truly in the southern wilderness. We hunted racoons on cold wintery nights, and I was surprised to find eating racoon was a delicious treat.

Through my grandmother's teachings to observe the environment, I watched how the leaders and managers assigned the tasks to the laborers in this new system. Clearly, this field system was tried and true, according to the field owners. The field owners owned the small grocery store near the field; of course, this was where you bought your lunch. You were even allowed to run a tab (have credit). So, they would pay you by the day, let's say $10.00. Snacks were provided at 10:00 am and 2:00 pm and you used the store for lunch. You were charged for the snacks, then you shopped at their store, so at the end of the day, you probably spent $8.00 leaving you with $2.00, and the field hands would go home happy. The farm owner just received free or close to free labor, which is pretty amazing. In this case, the trick to not participating in the system was to bring your food and snacks, claiming you were on a special diet. The last thing you needed to deal with was being seen as too good to comply. This strategy worked every time and allowed me to have special treatment. I was using the system against itself in a non-threatening way.

At the time I had no idea how powerful and beneficial these observations of systems would be later in life. I was just trying to exist with my analytical mind that was always racing. A large majority of the laborers had no original thought process of their own.

They were just individuals who worked for daily money. There was no inspiration to move up the leadership path. Working every day for day-money was all they wanted. I knew that working next to the lead, the work seemed to be a lot less, but the pay was a lot more. I understood leadership and management was the right place to be so I set out on learning what would it take to become the right-hand guy to the leader.

For example, in the tobacco field, the process was evolutionary. One planted the tobacco plant and then returned to the field to top the plant. This was a process of taking the tops off the plant to cause them to grow wide but not high. Once the plant was ready for picking, you cropped the plant. What cropping meant was taking off the bottom three leaves of the plant that were turning yellow. You accomplished this by sitting on the lowest seat of the tobacco harvester or, before the use of a harvester, you bent down and cropped the leaves. The harvester had four people cropping at one time. The harvester was pulled down through the tobacco field by a tractor. The tractor went up and down the rows of the tobacco field all day. The tobacco plant was picked and strung on a 1x1 inch stick that was about 3.5 feet long by what is called a stringer. When the stick was filled, then someone on the tractor would remove the stick and stack the filled sticks on a pallet that rode on the back of the harvester. Once the pallet was full, at the end of the row another individual would come up with a forklift and take the pallet off the harvester and put it on a truck. Once on the truck, then off to the barn the tobacco went. This is where tobacco was hung in a heated barn for a couple of weeks to dry out. Once the tobacco was dry, it was removed from the barn and put in burlap sacks to be sent off to the market for sale. At the market or big warehouses, your tobacco was graded and place in a row according to the quality and then the auctioneer would know where to start the auction price for your tobacco. Either low or high-grade tobacco you received the price for what it auctioned for during the process.

As a field worker, the first two processes were a must. You had to be a part of the planting and topping to be recognized as someone who knew what they were doing. Some of the field hands took pride in being good at knowing these processes. The natural progression in the field, if you were a go-getter like me, was to go from cropping to filling the pallet on the harvester, and then going to the barn to hang the tobacco. At the barn, you only worked when tobacco showed up to be hung, so you had thirty or forty-five-minute breaks per hour because of the delivery of the tobacco from the fields. So, I was inspired to get to the barn. Once I made that move happen, then I worked hard and the leadership saw and made me the assistant field leader. Others in the field showed no interest in taking on more responsibility. Despite the increase in pay, staying as a worker bee was appealing to them. As the assistant leader, I got to tell everyone else what to do and hold everyone accountable (in the tobacco system).

I also took jobs at the local Dairy Queen and the Tasty Freeze. While navigating these systems, I met with a few challenges understanding authority in business. The authority were the business owners who had relatives—the bank owner, the judge, lawyers, etc. Once you understood not to piss anyone off, then you were granted (not in writing) permission to move about the various jobs. You had to be seen as a non-threat. Because my Grandmother was a large landowner within the city, if someone confronted me, such as the business owner or the banker, all I had to say was I was Allen Green's Grandson and the seas were parted for me. I was very lucky to be in this position as a young man. She schooled me on how the system worked, and of all my siblings, and as the youngest, my grandmother saw I was receiving her advice, so she put her energies into me. I took what she said to heart and I watched what she did. My siblings did not follow the same advice. My grandmother had a very strong presence in this little town and no one wanted to get crossed up with her. She was well respected. I understood the value of being respected and would carry that into my future as I ambitiously navigated my next calling. It was not lost on me that I had been brought to this town under the care of my grandmother to make something of myself.

Field authority was far different than corporate authority. Everyone should work in the fast food industry or work in similar types of jobs at least once in their career to learn about the workforce. I believe the purpose of these kinds of jobs is two-fold. One, to train the workforce about a nine-to-five working environment; and two, to teach individuals about life and the levels of leadership you can achieve if you put effort into your actions. The understanding I gained from these two examples assisted me with deciding the direction I wanted to go in life. Neither of these choices would give me the level of knowledge needed to move in the right direction in life. I knew then that working at either one of those places was not my future. I knew to work in the fields was not my future either, so once again, I had to get out of the South.

As far as social entertainment in the small town of Baxley, there were two nightclubs. One nightclub was called the Ponderosa, which was for the younger crowd. The other club was called Maybelle's, where most of your parents' friends hung out, which made it the least likely place for younger folk to go, not wanting to have to be on their best behavior.

The Ponderosa was a no-holds-barred kind of place. There was no age limit to get in there so no limits on what could happen inside in the club. In terms of drugs and alcohol, the club was notorious for having fights or out-of-towners coming down and getting into altercations and sometimes shootings. The alcohol sold there was the cheapest around. The owner would buy the alcohol in bulk and sell brown whiskey or white whiskey (the cheapest on the market) in plastic cups. So you ordered your drink as a dollar shot. If you had the money, you could participate. This was the base of the system to keep poor people poor. There was no one talking about improving their education to find a better job. It was all about what tobacco or vegetable field you are going to work in to earn minimum pay.

These clubs were the hottest places in town to go to as a young kid. Again, now being exposed to girls, alcohol, and drugs, there were no holds barred; you could do anything you wanted if you did it within the walls of the club. Not a place I would recommend for the faint of heart! My first time going there I was about fourteen years old. It was certainly not endorsed by my mom. My brothers and sisters were patrons, so they were sort of watching over me while I was there. They were up to their own no-good activities, so it wasn't like I had someone truly watching over me. I look back on this experience as one of those unique insights into a kind of life where the Southern people were just filling up time and wallowing in lack of inspiration.

It was critical to recognize the slow, un-concerning system I was in during this time in my life. The people I dealt with were carefree and uneducated. To them, the cool thing was going to this club. They didn't see who the owner of this club, who was a black man was taking everything they had as far as money, intellect, and time. His system was simple: He was one of the only games in town, and he provided a false sense of security in this club. His prices matched the field hand and local minimum wage worker income. He sold alcohol by the cup so you could buy a $.50 shot or a $1.00 shot. This booze was very cheap, but the clientele didn't care, they could afford this and get drunk. His system greased the palms of the local authorities. They never raided this club even though they had to know what was going on inside. As you can see, there are many little systems within the bigger system living in the south, and I believe this is no different in the rest of the country. In retrospect, the club owner saw the system and he took full advantage of it.

The real sad aspect of this situation is to this day some of the people I knew then are still in the same town making the same drunken trouble, and now their children are following their foot-steps. Most are still working for $10 to $12 an hour thinking this is a good deal and drinking their wages away. They could not and will not advance forward in life. Most have never furthered their education, if they are even still alive. Although the Ponderosa burned down, the laziness in some of the people still exist.

The southern school system was so behind it was unbelievable. Uneducated people in an environment with drugs and alcohol? You can guess the outcome, and it was never anything positive. Reflecting back to my beginning of high school, I was so ready to just give up. I was only fourteen when I decided to quit high school because of peer pressure. The little get-togethers with the boys, parties during the day, running off with the girls that were supposed to be in school, all made me think I'd rather be in the streets than in school. This broke my mother's heart.

"Son," she said to me one day. "I don't care what you do in life but please be like your siblings, they all graduated from high school. So at least do that for me."

I loved my mom and didn't want her to be unhappy but I was pretty dead set against going back to school. I didn't care to compare myself to my siblings either. I had a little summer job for the city shoveling water from the side of the street, where runoff occurred when the workers were doing street repairs. I was getting paid minimum wage and I worked hard. I had a visiting relative who came to town from Connecticut. My mother asked him to talk to me and see if he could convince me to go back to school. He asked me what type of work I was doing, and I proudly told him I had a job with the city.

"Well, my friend," he said with a chuckle. "If you want to do this for the rest of your life, don't finish high school and this job will be the only thing you will be qualified to do."

Because I'm somewhat of an analytical person, when he said that to me I internalized his point of view a great deal and I knew shoveling water was not the future in store for me. My mom had done right by pushing me to see a different perspective. I don't know where I would be today had I not gone back to school the following year. I don't even want to conjecture, but I imagine it would have been a small future. I was fortunate to have the auto shop teacher take interest in me and offered me a job at the airport. He saw me as being diligent and honest. I didn't hang around with a lot of people. Back then I was more of an introvert, so I came off as someone smart and trustworthy. He invited me to come work for him at the local municipal airport. This was a major break-through. This made going back to school worth it for me. Before I got the airport job, I overcame some challenges which freed me to get cleared to work at the airport. The challenges were partying all night, leaving the club or someone's home and heading straight to work at the Dairy Queen. In most cases, still drunk from the night before. That wasn't going to fly for airport work.

Work on the farm was always present. In the morning before leaving for school we had to go and do the disgusting job of slop-ping the pigs. What that meant was all the garbage you saved over the evening and over a couple of days was put it in a bucket and you took that bucket down the pigs. While in school, sometimes our pigs would get out of the pen. We were allowed to leave school in the middle of the day to chase our pigs back to the farm and put them back in their pen. The school was about three-quarters of a mile from our farm.

This crazy farm living was balanced with working at the airport, which was a joy. I learned how to be a mechanic working on airplanes, and eventually how to fly. My boss, the pilot Bruce, and the owner of the airport, Harry Hardee, used to tell me I would be the first Black crop duster in the south if I stuck with them. This was a perfect example of being in the middle of a great system that was inviting me in, but I did not have the right glasses on to see what was going on around me. If I had recognized that system opportunity, life could have been different. I could have become a fighter pilot in the military, a commercial airline pilot, or worked in some other role in the aviation community. Instead, my mind was focused on getting out of Georgia as opposed to seeing what was around me. I learned how to change brakes, change out a magneto, service aircraft, and then fly aircraft at a young age. Unfortunately, I did not realize how beneficial this knowledge was to me. In retrospect, in learning the system, I did not realize I had been invited to the most prestigious aspect of the system in the South. The owner of the airport was definitely hardwired into the local business owners, the bankers, and so forth and so on. Proximity to him put me in a power position, and I could have written my ticket if I had chosen to stay in the South. I never had a father who sat me or my siblings down to share with us about life challenges or to recognize opportunity. So, I didn't recognize the opportunity in front of me working at the airport, but I did discover Rule of the System #1 which I would implement through the rest of my life: *Seek, Identify and appreciate your mentors. They have been put in your life to push you to greatness.*

The Navy excited me more, and it was a way out of the south. So, a career in aviation ended quickly right after high school.

I'm sure after college I could have gone back and become a city official of some sort, but since I didn't understand all the perks of being a part of this system, I missed that opportunity. The system is unforgiving; either you see it or you don't. I will repeat this fact many times throughout this book because of its importance. Once you have earned trust within the system, you have to safeguard it dearly. I had that chance, but I don't regret my decision and I do appreciate being able to look back and see the system I was in and where I was in the system. I was able to recognize later in other similar systems the good position I was in so I didn't miss future opportunities. This led to the understanding and enforcement of Rule of the System #2: *Stay focused on the objective and continuously re-evaluate your game plan.*

I joined the Navy as a torpedoman's mate under the delayed entry program in 1976. Looking back, I completely understand and never regret any of my decisions because they all taught me my next moves in life. Living in Georgia taught me a lot of valuable principles and a lot of basic necessities needed to survive. The most important aspect of this lifestyle was how it motivated me to do better.

After being exposed to several facets of the system, from farmhand to pilot, I realized I had a hunger to see more of the world than just the South. I didn't want to get stuck there around a majority of unmotivated people. Kind people like the airport owner showed me I had a lot of promise. So, off I went to discover a better system not knowing exactly what I was looking for, but I knew it was something out there I had to learn. Once you have the mindset to look to see the various systems, then it allows you to pick and choose what system you want to be a part of at this time. I developed Rule of the System #3: *Constantly survey the environment to ensure every day you see where you are at,* and it kept me out of harm's way. In my life, I use the fence concept. The fence concept is you either live on one side or the other. You cannot straddle the fence. You can't live on the left side and play on the right side or vice versa. You have to choose which side of the fence you're going to live on, and that's the side you stay on.

PART II
Military Life: 22 Years in the U.S. Navy

5 ~ Boot Camp: The Light at the End of the Tunnel

In a hurry to change the environment that I was in, I borrowed my sister's car without her permission and drove to Brunswick, Georgia to join the U.S. Navy at seventeen years old. My mother and father signed the documents. Because I was still in high school in November 1976, I had to go into the delayed entry program and wait until after graduation. I graduated June 4, 1977 and entered the Navy on June 9, 1977. Less than one week later, I headed to boot camp. Orlando, Florida here I come! I entered boot camp with a chip on my shoulder and an attitude that embraced the militant movement and perspective of Malcom X, Eldridge Cleaver, and the likes of the Black Panthers. I had developed this attitude because I was in the South in the seventies and a lot of this civil rights mentality had held over from the sixties. I was the anti-system guy. It was us against them, whoever the "them" was. Better defined, I was a 1970s radical person, supporting the "power to the people" movement. I thought I had it going on with my mini afro.

My brothers (two had been in the Navy prior to me) had warned me that during boot camp, the establishment would try to scare you. So, I was not afraid when I entered into boot camp. I was able to roll with the punches. My childhood and teen years had set me up for surviving new systems, especially dysfunctional ones. My father had been a street hustler, but he was a good provider. My mother was just a plain old-fashioned hard-working woman who took care of seven children. The blessing was she had enough sense to teach us not to get caught up into the outside systems, meaning the penal systems. She took us to church, and used church as a way to instill good and bad into us. These religious gatherings exposed us to different aspects of society and spirituality, which is part of the reason why I believe most people miss the systems in front of them; it's due to their lack of exposure. The church was an early environment of morality for me. You have to have a keen sense of what the systems are to recognize the system you're in at any given time. Because of my childhood knowledge, I was able to recognize the various systems, which gave me a leg up in the Navy.

Arriving at boot camp, you are completely unconscious of what's around you. However, you do know you're in a military system. So, given that fact, your first option should be to figure out what is a military system. That should take all of about two seconds, and once you realize it, then you have to quickly abide by it. You truly only get a day to figure the system out. You're being observed from the moment you step off the bus until they make assignments of the leadership team within your company. You have to be smart, humble, and assertive all at the same time to be recognized as someone mature enough to take a leadership role at a very young age. I adopted Rule of the System # 4 at this time: *Never become pompous or arrogant. Adversity is not the enemy; stay humble.* The way their system works is that you have a short amount of time to prove your worth. If you fail, you get fired immediately and lose the opportunity to become a leader while in boot camp. Boot camp is a very fast-moving system and does not have time to nurture you. Either you instinctively have the where-withal to show leadership and understand the military process or you don't. If you don't, that's okay because then you are just put with the average folks in the company. This is not necessarily a bad thing; it just says you're not ready for this particular system.

The company commander gathered all the section leaders and what we call the Recruit Chief Petty Officer (RCPO), and he would give us directions he wanted us to follow. You didn't have to *like* what he said, you just had to *do* what he said. I understood that you needed to put your pride in your pocket and keep your opinion to yourself. From this understanding, I solidified Rule of the System #5: *It is not important to always win; let others win.*

They would say to us, an opinion is like a butthole; everyone has one and they all stink. As rude as this may sound, it was good advice. I stayed to myself, I did what I was told, and within the first week I was selected to be a section leader for the remaining seven weeks. I quickly learned again how being a part of the chain of command and not being considered one of the masses grant-ed privileges that offset the orders and actions you had to take, whether you liked them or not. As a section leader, we didn't have to do all the things everyone else had to do. I saw the system and process of boot camp, and paid keen attention to staying in good graces within it.

We were among the only boot camps with a co-ed environ-ment. We got to see girls the entire time in boot camp. Sometimes we even got to say hello, and during mealtimes we could have a quick conversation with them. Those small interactions kept me going. Life was good, except for the fourth week when I called home and talked to my eldest niece. She was asking me when was I going to come home and how she loved and missed me. The fact that my niece made me aware of being away from home made me a little homesick. This gripped my heart and brought tears to my eyes. I was laying in my bunk later that evening when I realized I had institutionalized myself. I panicked a little. I did not know what to expect in the future. I knew I was into something I could not quickly get out of, so I had to subdue my anxieties and try to understand how to survive for the next several weeks.

What I quickly learned was the boot camp system was not racial; it was not about black and white; it was about life. This was a critical element of the system. The system did not see a color, nor did it see money. The system saw only processes and people working within or without. It was just that simple. I wasn't necessarily afraid of the gamesmanship and the things that were going to happen in boot camp. But what I did learn was how there was a pecking order, and so I watched who was being selected for various positions. The system's pecking order is not hierarchical; it is time-based.

I'll never forget a recruit, let's call him James. James decided he was going to build his little congregation inside of the already-established one. He was going to have a certain group follow him despite the direction the sanctioned group was following.

One night James received a blanket party. A blanket party is *not* the kind of party you want! A blanket party is when a bunch of guys wait until you are sound asleep, and then they throw a blanket over top your entire body and hold it down tight. Why? Because then they beat you with bars of soap in socks or with their fist or anything in their hands. Imagine being awakened from a nice beautiful dream by a bunch of guys beating you all over your body. By the time James realized what was going on, all the guys raced back, jumped in their racks, and pretended like they were sleeping. So, James wakes up in a dark compartment, beaten, bruised, disoriented, and no idea what just happened to him. James had to go to the dentist the next morning because his teeth were knocked loose.

James was introduced to the Navy system. He learned how the team was heading in one direction and he was either going to go in that direction or be beaten into it. The interesting part of this was that this blanket party was given to James by all the other section leaders, including the RCPO and myself. After James' medical conditions were taken care of, he was returned to our unit, but he was a changed man. Reflecting on this event, it was an affirmation of succumbing to the system of the military—it's what you had to do. Personally, being a part of this event didn't bother me because it wasn't me getting the beat-down. I was a conformist in order to survive. James was introduced to and broken down by the system.

This was a perfect scenario of how systems work. We were all new to the Navy and none of us knew anything about blanket parties. Our instructor, the company commander, sat us down and told us how blanket parties occur and typically who received them. He did not authorize us to conduct a blanket party; he just told us what blanket parties were. James was building his own personal fiefdom inside of an established system. Now, of course, you have young, eager minds who were just told about blanket parties and how they work and how effective they are in making people cooperate with the established system. We, the leadership, got together and discussed this blanket party and the strategic application of using it. We identified James as a threat to the system and the system either had to make him conform or eradicate him from the system. As part of the group that saw him as a problem, I had to make the determination to participate. The way this was planned, only trusted individuals were told and it was kept at the section leaders level and higher. We all knew the system could turn on us if we didn't abide by the rules. The blanket party was the first option. James was given the blanket party, everyone was involved, and those who were not went radio silent. Because there were no witnesses, this event didn't happen, so it was written off as if James slipped in the showers. James received a 100% full dosage of the system and how it can turn against you. After the blanket party, James became one of the best sailors in our company. In life, when public figures or powerful people decide they're bigger than the system, the system humbles them and takes them down.

Just as I had done in the tobacco fields, I survived boot camp and our company graduated with honors. We won a lot of the competitive awards given in boot camp, such as best marching company. Now it was time to put all of what we had learned about the Navy through the test. The test is called real life in the Navy. While leaving bootcamp was a joy, the next chapter ahead of me was scary. The unknown awaiting me. Armed with a few Rules of the System, I was ready. Or so I thought.

6 ~ MY FIRST DUTY STATION: THE NEW BEGINNING

My first Duty station was located at 32nd Street Naval Base in San Diego, California. I was going on board the USS Dixie AD-14. The USS Dixie was a Destroyer Tender class ship and the oldest active naval ship at this time. She even had wooden decks. This class of ships is no longer in the U.S. Navy. My arrival date was December 7, 1977 and a day I will always remember. December 7 is Pearl Harbor day. I crossed the quarterdeck as sharp as I could possibly be, straight out of boot camp with visions of grandeur, heading into the future. Dixie turned out to be the best ship I ever served on. It had a family-like environment and the men genuinely cared for each other.

However, from December 7 until Christmas that year, there were three major incidents. A guy I served with in my shop stole a weapon from the shop, went to downtown San Diego, and committed suicide. The next incident was a friend who got upset because someone looked at his car, and he shot them three times in the heart. Lastly, in the shop's Armory, two guys I served with were playing around and one shot the other. At this point, I was ready to resign and go home. Was this what life would be like in the military? I had to question myself. People dying all around me? I couldn't believe I had committed myself to this organization. I was not thinking these three incidents had nothing to do with real Navy life. Now was the first awaking to the system on board the ship of what was not my system. The system did have unforeseen situations occur.

These were situations where someone else's system went wrong, not mine, and I was an observer to their system as opposed to being in the real system around me. Regarding the first incident, the guy was a squirrel and unstable. His roommate was totally insensitive to his death, only being upset because he killed himself before rent was due.

In the incident in the armory, the horseplay guys shouldn't have had guns out at all, or they were not conducting safe gun handling procedures. They were assigned a task and here they were playing John Wayne during working hours. Lastly, the new friend who shot the other guy and killed him, well I believe he was from Chicago or New York or some major city and truly had a chip on his shoulder and thought he was really a mutineer. I learned this behavior was not the Navy and so I was okay. I focused on my career a little, but I still had my own chip. I did enjoy getting into fights to defend my honor, or so I thought. Luckily, I was never caught doing anything wrong, therefore my career stayed intact.

One of the blessings was how senior enlisted personnel would see something in a young sailor and take it upon himself to become their mentor. In the Navy, the unofficial, un-codified, mentorship system is called having a "Sea Daddy." The gentlemen that pulled me aside in the torpedo shop of the Destroyer Tender, the USS Dixie AD-14, was named Albert McCoy.

"Young fella," he said to me, "you're not going to get very far with that chip on your shoulder. There's a system that's been in place for over 200 years and your little black butt is not going to change it. So, you need to get with the program or get off the bus."

What he meant then by the "system" was the U.S. Navy, which has processes and procedures in place for obvious reasons. In order for the military to be a strong fighting force, the rules have to be followed strictly, and he was talking about that very system. I had no idea then that I would enter a kind of master's program in my life of these systems. Without someone guiding you in the early stages of your career or in life, you will be flailing in the wind.

At least with their guidance, you have a chance of survival. They will encourage you to take the right actions and show you the steps you need to take to get promoted. They teach you the proper attitude to have and what the United States Navy is all about. And they will also let you know what your responsibilities are. Therefore, it was prudent to sit back and be a student as opposed to being a know-it-all. Again, Rules of the System #4 and #5 applied: *Never become pompous or arrogant. Adversity is not the enemy; stay humble* and *It is not important to always win; let others win.*

Regarding my own Sea Daddy, I initially hated him. He was tough on me. He did not give me any slack, but he saw something I didn't see in me. He would call me aside and select me to do all the dirty work. He would do that just to see what my reaction would be, and there were always lessons to be learned. My Sea Daddy saw how I had been introduced to a system and he took it upon himself to enhance my knowledge of the system. He took me under his wing and brought clarity into my life. He showed me what was important to get involved with and not to get involved with, the people to hang around with and the people not to hang around with at any time. I clearly learned about the old adage of *birds of a feather flock together*. There is a tremendous amount of truth to that saying. Little did I know it then, but later in life I figured it out. He would ask me to go out to dinner with him instead of hanging out with the boys. As a child growing up, my parents used to say, the medicine doesn't taste good, but it is good for you. In this example, my Sea Daddy was stern and didn't have room for playtime. I fought this with a passion. I'd rather be hanging out with the boys getting into mischief versus getting a life lesson. Once again, though, with him I was in good hands. With the boys, who knew what would happen. I didn't see it at the time. He was a good man, a good father, a good father figure, and a good teacher.

When I reflect on what Albert McCoy did for me, I want to go and hug his neck. He taught me the rule of the game: *Seek, identify, and appreciate your mentors. They have been put in your life to push you to greatness.*

It took a lot of patience and courage for him to take the time with me to teach me what the system was about, how it operated, and the rules of the game. He saw in me how I was able to handle what he was teaching me. There were others around us who I know he tried to reach out to, but they did not get it and they ran away to continue to do the things they were doing that were not conducive to the good order and discipline of the system.

I met a guy named Brad who I thought was a friend. We had a lot in common and he understood what I had been going through with my McCoy teachings. As time passed, and with my wife Diane telling me about his character, I realized he was not who I thought I had known for all those years. As a matter of fact, I met him shortly after leaving McCoy and today, forty-something years later, he's worse off now. And I think the main reason for this is because he never took the time to understand the system around him. I witnessed early on how the system had embraced him they were raising him up in the system, but he let other distractions cloud his vision on the benefits the system had to offer. Four wives and six children later, he was out of work for almost ten years. Now he's back to work working for minimum wages in his sixties. The system does not see color; it does not see money; it is what it is, and you have to understand what it is.

There's an adage that says *believe nothing you hear and half of what you see.* There's a lot of wisdom to this saying, and especially when it involves the system. I learned how to keep my mouth shut to keep my opinions to myself, and to understand how sometimes things were not what they appeared to be. I also learned to take advantage of good fortune (initially introduced to me by my grandmother). I've learned over time how the gamesmanship that's played continues sends you on wild goose chases to distract you from what's going on. And if you are one of these people who listens to respond, then you will miss the boat. I've learned over time there are two types of listeners: One who listens to respond and the other who listens to hear. Navigating through the system successfully means you must learn to listen to hear because remember, you have to listen to what's *not being said.* I learned later in life the more senior I became, the fewer words were used, but the process was more impactful. It's about listening to what's not being said, and reserving my judgments or opinions allows the system to unveil itself almost 100% of the time.

The system amazes me. Why? Because it's been around forever, and you can start to see how successful people become more successful because they follow the rules of the systems they are in.

I began to advance my education of the system on board USS Dixie, and as my time in the Navy progressed at each duty station, my knowledge was enhanced more and more. By the time I was ready to be commissioned as an officer, I had a good foundation of what the system was and how to play in the system.

One day, onboard Dixie, it was about 3:45 pm in the afternoon and almost time to shut down the shop and go home.

"Hey Maxwell," my mentor called out.

"Hey what?" And the minute I responded that way, I knew my answer was wrong.

"How about you go and get a vacuum cleaner and go down five decks below in the weapons magazine in the shop on the ship and clean out around all the scuttles within the hatches."

I was horrified and upset. It was 3:45 pm and there was no way in the world I could get this done in fifteen minutes and he knew it and didn't care. He said do it. So, I got the vacuum cleaner out and I went down five decks below and started at the lowest deck. I was beyond upset. Every level I cleaned I was cursing him under my breath and watching the clock as time ticked by. Oh, I believe by the time I was finished it was about 7:00 pm in the evening, too late to do anything. But guess what, McCoy was still there watching me. Finally, I completed my tasks.

"Hey mister smart-mouth," he said to me. "I was calling to ask you to go out to dinner. Because of your flippant response you needed a lesson."

I didn't understand it then and it didn't make matters better, but I later learned to understand exactly what happened. That was just one of many things he would do. I remember one time riding with him to dinner and there was some music playing on the car radio. I believe it was a song by Betty Wright, an oldie but goodie and as the song is playing, boy he was all into this music. After the song was over, he sat me down and explained to me what the song was all about. The song was about managing a good relationship. She sang about how you deal with the good and bad to make a relationship survive. At that time, I could care less.

You see, being a young fool, you can miss all those golden nuggets. The good thing was how I was an analytical person. I would internalize experiences and go back later and ask myself what he was talking about. More importantly, why he was talking to me and wanted me to understand. How about that transformation—it was happening right before my eyes.

"I will be so glad when I transfer away from you," I said to him one day, teasing but also serious.

"May 25th 1981 will be the day you will graduate the school of life," he said.

I had no idea what he was talking about until I learned it was the date he was going to retire from the United States Navy, and he wouldn't be around anymore to guide me.

During this time in my life, a lot was going on. It was being new to the Navy, surviving boot camp, and having people close to me die. But having someone take an interest in me certainly raises suspicion. You want to know why. Why me? This is a question that may never be openly or verbally answered, but I know and I believe we all have a destination and a purpose, and an Albert McCoy who was the angel who guided me during this time of my life. I don't think anyone else could have reached me as he did. I had a lot of respect for him, and he carried himself very well.

There were others on board the ship in my department at his same level, but I had little or no respect for them, or they didn't strike me as someone who could give me sound advice. Albert was an individual with strong values and some very deep critical thinking skills. He was a man from Kansas City who made his way to California and joined the Navy and overcame the challenges in front of him. I'm so grateful for Albert McCoy.

My experience in the Navy made me mature in a rapid fashion. I had to learn tough lessons early in life as a young man. I had to learn how it was all about my intentions and consequences. No one else was at fault if things went good or bad when I made choices. Rule of the System #6 was born: *Own your mistakes but don't take the fall for others.*

Either you reap the benefits or suffer the consequences of your actions. And my friend ensured I knew this very well. He was a good man and he saw something in me I didn't know I had, but I'm so glad he did see it in me. I am who I am today because of him.

The time with him soon came to an end and I was leaving Dixie. I transferred to Norfolk, Virginia in 1979 to go on board the USS Shenandoah AD-26, which was another Destroyer Tender. The difference being this was now the East Coast Navy versus the West Coast. At this time, I had heard there were these different Navies. I heard the East Coast was a stricter Navy than the West Coast. The reason for this was because it was close to the Washington D.C. area, meaning there was more oversight from the upper leadership.

7 ~ USS SHENANDOAH: SHAPING THE MAN

Arriving to the new ship brought about changes. The nickname for the USS Shenandoah was the Shannon Doper. Drugs were rampant on board the ship. A U.S. Navy vessel with such drug issues, most people do not realize these types of activities happen in the Navy. While overseas it was very easy to get drugs, and on the ship it wasn't very strict. We had a couple of guys get busted for buying camel poop while overseas, thinking it was hash. I was flashed right back to Philly gangster-style living. A kind of homecoming, but lacking any festivity or nostalgia. I had been spoiled on board the great ship Dixie and the family-like environment I became comfortable living in.

Because of the lessons I had learned in the previous naval system, I knew to look for the good guys to hang out with on the Shenandoah, and there were a few. I naturally gravitated toward them. Knowing how to find good people in a new environment is critical if you want to go places. Although someone may look cool or be fun to be around, they could be a major disaster in your life. They may be just existing, not really living, and to live you have to thrive in your environment and understand the system or systems you are in. If you violate the system rules or do not pay attention to the rules, then the system is unforgiving, and it waits for no one.

I didn't have a Sea Daddy on board the Shenandoah, but my lessons and teachings were all set thanks to the astute guidance of Albert McCoy. I knew the do's and don'ts and the rights and wrongs—the systems of how Navy ship politics worked. In some cases, rather than sound the alarm and ratting someone out, being a new guy to the ship, I had to earn the new system's trust. Therefore, I couldn't make waves too early. There's a time when to insert yourself, and when you do, make sure you are 100% accepted in the system. Make sure you're heard by the systems players, and you are respected by them all. Here is where I discovered the implementation of Rule of the System #7: *Never be too demanding.* It was supported by Rule # 3: *Constantly survey the environment to ensure every day you see where you are at.*

As you can see, the more my life unfolds and offers new systems and experiences, I lean on the seven rules I have thus far created to survive.

Early in my Navy career, I had a major chip on my shoulder. I thought I could change what I thought was not right in the Navy. I was talking to a guy one day and he was very straight with me. He said, "My friend, there's a system in place and has been in place for over 200 years," he said, "and your little black butt isn't going to change it." This was the second time I heard this comment about the system. Therefore, you need to get with the program or else the program will get rid of you. That was the best advice I could have ever received because that's when the system truly became real to me and I knew I had to understand what I was up against. It's not that the system wasn't real earlier, but now I was getting into Navy politics and it was certainly a skillful art you had to learn if you wanted to progress. With Navy politics, you could have one person destroy your whole career with the stroke of a pen. That person was your supervisor. The worst thing you could ever do is be overwhelmingly tough. The reason why is because you have no integrity, because you'll do anything to get ahead, and your supervisor knows that's a dangerous place for someone to be. There can be no trust in you. Rule of the System #8 sprung forth for me at this time: *Be flexible to change but stand your ground ethically.* Stand on your own merits to understand leadership's direction, embrace it, and then you will do great in that system.

I was a member of the weapons department and the internal special weapons group, having received this designation right out of boot camp. We were a special, isolated group of people. We did not typically associate with other members of the ship, officers and enlisted, because of the nature of our weapons handling procedures and top secret information we dealt with on a daily basis. Intermingling with the rest of the crew would compromise the sensitive nature of our operations. So, hanging around the right people on board was paramount. Due to my nuclear weapons affiliation, my group was even smaller than ever. I couldn't talk about what I did to anyone except fellow weapons shipmates on the ship. We worked behind locked doors. We always had to wear a badge around our necks for identification to access our spaces. In some cases a dosimeter monitored the personal levels of radiation you might have received at any given time. You were only allowed a certain level of radiation in a certain period of time. Once again I was too young and uninformed to fully realize or understand what I was doing working with and around nuclear weapons and how critical it was doing the sensitive things to the weapons we did. The program I was in was called the personal reliability program. As a member, I wasn't allowed to have any personal problems with money, alcohol or drugs, mental instability, or anything that questioned your character or integrity. At the time when all this was happening in my life, I had no idea that this was all part of the shaping and building process that was making me the man who I became. I simply implemented Rule of the System #2: *Stay focused on the objective and continuously re-evaluate your game plan.* I'm so thankful I was open-minded enough to receive all this learning and information. I'm also glad I was level-headed enough to not let anything too excessive happen in my life, and I was able to see the benefits of being a part of this program.

On the Shenandoah, my new really good friend was a guy named Kenneth Gordon, AKA Flash Gordon. Flash was from Atlanta, Georgia, so I knew how most Georgia people think, which made it easy for us to get along. He was a very funny guy, and we were very similar. I learned through this friendship experience Rule of the System #9: *Stay close to your circle, which should be extremely small (1 or 2).* We knew about the country life the about the farm way of life. I knew about the city life too, and talking about it intrigued Flash. Because we got along so well, we got into deviant trouble together. I could trust him and he could trust me. You see, back on the Dixie, I honed my skills in martial arts. I was a pretty good fighter, so on board the Shenandoah, and of course with the East Coast gangster mentality, I was okay in a rough environment. I was young and dumb to the fullest. Flash, on the other hand, was just a strong country boy who didn't think much, so he was a great partner. He didn't mind fighting as long as I was with him. Flash used his brute strength to overcome any situation. Flash wasn't analytical or very thoughtful. All brawn, no brains.

While on board the Shenandoah, the ship was deployed in March, 1979. On the East Coast it is called a Med Cruise (Mediterranean Cruise). On the West Coast, it's called a West Pac (Western Pacific). This was my first cruise on board a naval vessel going overseas. Back then when the ship set sail and was underway from the docks, all your information or communication flow to the United States disappeared. We didn't have email, we didn't have Facebook and all the modes of communication used today. Back then, you received letters from family friends, and anyone you wrote would hopefully write you back. It was pretty critical during those days to receive a letter as this was part of your sanity check and calming force to help you cope with being away from home. Every day there was a mail call. The men stood around like hungry wolves waiting on a letter. I used to write to anyone and everyone. All I wanted was a letter back from someone.

After about three or four weeks at sea, our first port of call was in Naples, Italy. When we arrived, Flash and I and other friends decided to go explore the city. The first place to head to was the red-light district and the off-limits area. Naples was a beautiful city and Italy was a beautiful country. The people were wonderful, the food was good, but all we could think about was chasing the young ladies. Forget about all the beauty of the city or appreciating all the historical, cultural, and architectural features. There were Italian girls!

After enjoying Naples for about 45 days, we went to Trieste, Italy and several other Italian cities. At the port entrance of most sites, the panhandlers are on the side of the streets selling crappy merchandise for cheap prices. You were in Italy, so you bought it. You would buy the gold rings that looked very nice, but by the time you got back to the ship, your finger would already be turning green. Or you would buy a suede coat or jacket and within two weeks the suede would rub off. I mean this stuff was cheaper than cheap, so the combination of being young, dumb, and in a foreign country it all collided together. Bad decisions were always the results. One night, we got ourselves in a pickle. While by now in my life I fully understood Rule of the System #3: *Constantly survey the environment to ensure every day you see where you are at*, I didn't adhere to it. Sometimes, your lessons are not complete and you need one more tangle with trouble.

We were told on the ship before leaving to never go around any political rallies or events. Deviant by nature and after drinking about eight to ten bottles of vino (wine) that we stole from a local restaurant, Flash and I with a few other friends ended up right in the center of a political rally. Imagine American sailors in the middle of an Italian political rally. We were setting ourselves up for major disaster. If we had been spotted as being involved in the politics behind this rally, an international incident could have occurred, which is a very big deal. Somehow, we were smart enough to get out of the situation without getting caught or getting involved or noticed. I learned Rule of the System #10: *Be discerning about whom you trust with your ambitions.* The next day with severe hangovers, we were able to laugh about the situation. This was just one example of the dumb things we did.

Our next stop was Barcelona, Spain. Flash and I were again out roaming the streets. Barcelona highlighted the Spanish culture with the old ruins, and the coliseum was a bucket list excursion. The local people there were very nice and kind. Flash and I met two beautiful young ladies. They convinced us they could exchange our money for a better exchange rate than what we saw on the streets or at the local exchange centers. Like the two smart guys we were (NOT), we gave them our money to get exchanged for a better rate, and of course they disappeared into a building and up a long flight of stairs. Flash and I knew where they went, and brains and brawn were about to attack the young ladies to get our money back. Flash and I devised our plan. We were going to race up the stairs and break into this room where they went and get our money back. We pumped each other up, we got all riled up and went to get our money, ignoring Rule of the System #7: *Never be too demanding*. We ran up the stairs and walked into this room instead of busting into the room. The girls were there and they had made the money exchange. They were amongst a bunch of their friends, talking and dancing. They did give us our money back at a good exchange rate as promised with no issues. After observing the room more closely, what we saw in that room were some guys three times our size that could have out-numbered and out-fought us I'm sure, so busting into this place trying to be tough guys could have led to our demise. The moral of that story is look before you leap.

There was a ton of experience gained during this cruise, especially about self-preservation and thinking before you act. The system has rules I knew must be followed. You always have to protect yourself; always thinking three steps ahead. You have to anticipate other actions and you have to anticipate the impacts actions will have on you. The beauty of knowing the system or being able to recognize the system certainly allows you to strategically act or to sit back and watch. I've watched so many people who have no clue about the system appear to have everything under control and then torpedo themselves. This happens all too often for people; they clearly do not understand how the process and the systems around them work. However, it is somewhat entertaining to watch this happen because I took the time to understand my circumstances and apply rules to the game.

We had a commitment to our government to be ambassadors, especially within our highly classified weapons group, which was a big responsibility at nineteen or twenty years old. The military made me mature fast, and without my mentor Albert around, I had to think for myself. We went to Palma de Mallorca Spain, the

French Riviera, Augusta Bay, and other ports in Spain and Italy. After five months, the fun was over and we were heading home. The year was 1979 and there were a lot of world events happening of which we were completely oblivious because once the ship pulled away from the docks, you were largely disconnected from all communications with the United States. Any information we received during the cruise was from shipmates who had an opportunity to go home and come back during the cruise, and of course we were all excited to hear about their adventures at home.

We returned to Norfolk Virginia in the late fall. Normally, when a ship returns from a six-month cruise, the ship remains in a three-section duty rotation until after the stand-down period (every three days you have to stay on the ship). The stand-down period gives the returning sailor time to re-enter their home after being gone for six months. It allows time for the families to gel and the spouses to adjust to not having to be both mom and dad. The work assignments are light and minimal. Normal duty rotation is a six-section (every six days you had duty, which means you couldn't leave the ship.) Because of all the drug problems during the cruise and enlisted men on restriction, we did not get that privilege. We immediately went back into six-section duty when we pulled into port. I was so glad to get off of the USS Shenandoah and no longer be aligned with the debauchery of the other sailors. It was a very interesting experience, but a side of the Navy that wasn't pleasant. This was all a part of the character molding.

My real transitions would truly begin now that I had cruise experience and a little more maturity. My eyes were opened a bit more, but I had hardly learned the lessons.

8 ~ TORPEDOMAN TRAINING IN CHARLESTON: MAKING ADULT DECISIONS

I t had to be the coldest winter morning ever in Norfolk—January 1, 1980. The temperature was bone-chilling cold. I wore about four layers of clothes, a three-quarter-length cashmere overcoat, and thermal underwear and was still freezing cold. I was finally leaving the USS Shenandoah and heading to Orlando, Florida where it would be warm. Orlando is where the Weapons, Nuclear Power and Electronic Technician technical schools were. All Torpedoman's mates did their training in Orlando. They had the various schools there from the beginners to the advanced. At this point in my career, I was in the middle stages of schooling. The schooling I was required to attend for my assignment included basic electricity and electronics, and Torpedoman C School (more advanced than A School or B School).

In Orlando, it was still all about having fun and being a stereotypical sailor. I was young and single. This is the place where all the young girls were leaving boot camp and coming into the world changed and looking for a young man. The young people who were in C School were looking to get into relationships because they felt they were mature now as the Navy afforded them that perspective and idea. I had the privilege in this go-round, which was my second time in Orlando, to have a better appreciation for what the Navy had to offer me. The first time I was just out of boot camp—very new and very green - I was relegated to the base. I was an E3 in rank (a non-Petty Officer), the low man on the totem-pole.

Now that I was a rank higher (an E4 Petty Officer), I had more money, leadership responsibility, and common sense, so I was able to buy my first car and explore beyond the base. It made me enjoy the tour differently. I bought a 1970 Buick LeSabre. This car was extremely awesome and in showroom condition. The original owner bought the car new and took great care of it. Back then you put plastic seat coverings over all the seats to keep them clean, so the upholstery in his car was perfect. The car ran like a well-oiled sewing machine. Like a dreamboat, it floated in the air. Back then they were making heavy cars, and this LeSabre four-door was a big car. Being a young sailor with a car of this caliber certainly turned heads. Having a ride like this, I didn't have a problem dealing with the young ladies. Because of my availability and having a nice ride, I was very picky about what girls or guy friends I choose to talk to or associate with while stationed there. I remembered Rule of the System #9: *Stay close to your circle, which should be extremely small (1 or 2).*

Orlando was a party place for a bunch of young sailors with youthful energy, all looking for the hook-up, because that's what we did back then. A sailor's delight was to party all night. I was doing well in school, I was doing well in the Navy, so I had no complaints. I had not thought through my future objectives with a woman. So, my criteria was mainly their beauty and an attraction. I had not built any kind of moral code and I was not a very caring individual. I met a young lady by the name of Marie who had black hair and pretty blue eyes. She was white, from Boston,

Massachusetts. When I first saw Marie, I said to her, you are so beautiful and I'd love to take you out on a date. Without hesitation, she agreed to meet the following night. The next night came and went and I did not look for Marie. As a matter of fact, I intentionally did not look for Marie. A few days passed and I ran into her.

"How dare you stand me up?" she said with a vehement annoyance.

I was shocked and stunned because when I said all those kind words to her I wasn't really sure if she was serious. I told her this fact and we finally went out on a date.

We had a wonderful time, and from that point forward we were inseparable. We both were in school. She was doing well I was doing well, and it was time to start thinking about our next duty assignments. School was coming to a close, so I told Marie I was going to be stationed in Charleston, South Carolina.

"I have a surprise for you," she said. "I am being stationed in Charleston with you."

I was amazed at our luck, but she was leaving about two weeks after me, so once again I didn't take our moving there together very seriously. She was not my focus. Rule #2: *Stay focused on the objective and continuously re-evaluate your game plan.* I was headed to a new duty station and that was my number one priority.

I drove to Charleston and started working. Lo and behold maybe two-and-a-half or three weeks later Marie showed up and checked in to the shop where we ended up working together. Initially, Marie lived in the barracks. I had an apartment out in town. She would come to visit every now and then and I decided that we should move in together. Imagine if you will, in 1980 Charleston South Carolina, an African American man and a gorgeous white woman living together. Having spent time in Georgia, I was a little bit gun-shy of the racism. Whether it was real or perceived, I feared it would be an issue. We never let it restrict us from our travels, nor did we ever have any issues out in town. Living in Charleston was like living in the country with an attitude. There were the country folks that lived outside of the Navy base areas, and then there were the city slickers from the Navy.

In our shop it was a different story while stationed there. At first I didn't see it, but later it came to light. There was a certain level of racism going on. Racial issues were not prevalent on the Navy base, so it became much more obvious in the shop where we worked. Rule of the System #3 was in full play: *Constantly survey the environment to ensure every day you see where you are at.*

Being back in the South in a mixed relationship screwed my perspective up with the system. I anticipated blatant racism and I didn't see it, but I did see the unspoken words and actions of racism. The stealthy type systems are especially critical to recognize. These are the systems I've never spoken or talked about, but you know they're there because things happen. And if you're not aware, then by the time you do figure it out, all the damage has been done and it cannot be undone. So I'm so thankful for my prior understanding and knowledge of the system. You hear people say it's not personal, it's just business, but it *is* personal, and it *is* business if it impacts you. But if you understand how the system works, you will be able to separate the personal from the business, and when you're able to do that, you'll be able to navigate and manage the system around you. Rule of the System #11: *Don't take anything personally. This is a waste of your time* became a strong component of how I worked through my various environments from this time forward. The stealthy systems are the ones that are most challenging to deal with while in the midst of them.

Nonetheless, it is a system and it can be dealt with while it's in operation. That's the beauty of being aware of the system.

Half of the people in the shop favored Marie. The ones who favored Marie were the ones who did not like the fact she was dating a black man and did not like me. The other half accepted me and accepted her because they didn't care about our mixed situation.

After Marie and I started living together, my performance started going down to 3.4–3.6. Up to this point, my Navy career was outstanding. I consistently received 4.0 evaluation marks. Nothing had changed in me or my performance. I was the same sharp guy I always had been. The only difference was there was now an overshadowing of the racial tensions within the people in the torpedo shop we served in. Charleston itself as a town was not obviously racist like what I had experienced living in Georgia. Yet, the torpedo shop had people from all walks of life who would surprise me by being racist. I dealt with it I and did not let it affect me. I applied Rule of the System #8: *Be flexible to change but stand your ground ethically.* Marie also had a dark side to her. She talked about fighting with the devil. She believed that fight to be real and the way she would talk about it sometimes scared me.

One day, Marie told me about a drug deal she wanted me to help her orchestrate. Up to this point, I had no idea she was deep into dealing drugs. Because I really cared for her, she and I, with a few other so-called friends, put together a plan. We would buy a bunch of pot from a known bad guy. I always carried two weapons, either a 9mm on my side and a .357 under the front seat of my car. Sometimes I would switch them up. Going along with Marie's plan we headed over to this guy's house. We get there and the guy was being cool. A little too cool for my comfort. The deal starts going down, but this guy starts getting a little nervous, so I pulled my gun out on him. I took his money and his drugs. Marie and the other were egging this on, so I had to show toughness. Inside I was terrified. We leave his place and head back to our apartment. On the drive back they were telling me how much of a rebel I was and that I was the man. Of course, I couldn't show that my nerves were shot and the thought of what had just happened scared the crap out of me.

We get to the apartment and Marie is hugging me telling me how proud she was of me. For the remainder of the evening, there was a lot of drinking and trash being talked about. Little did any of them know what I was thinking. What if I had pulled the trigger and shot that guy? The thought of going to jail was horrifying. After this incident, I knew my circle of friends needed to change. I realized after this event that none of my so-called friends would do anything to get me out of jail and my life would have been destroyed forever.

This was a defining time in my life. I had to choose my future direction.

The system is unforgiving. You can leverage the positives in the system or force yourself into the negatives of the system. In our country, we have various major systems around us. There's the welfare system, and there's the penal system, there is the education system, and many other systems out there. Let's do a snapshot of the penal system: This system is like a snake in the grass. It lays there and waits for you to make a mistake so it can swallow you whole. The rules, once you're in it, work in a way so you'll never get out of it, and you just became a second-rate citizen. This is by far one of the most dangerous systems in our culture. Most young people, particularly African American young men, do not understand the depth and power of the penal system. This system has a pre-entrance environment and then it has the entry environment. So the pre-entrance environment is getting young men to get caught up in gangs and all sorts of stupid things. You can try to warn young men about this system, but because the system has such a deep hold on you, they actually think in some cases it's a *privilege* to be caught up into that system. What they don't realize is that once in it, you can never get out of it.

The alternative to hanging out with my current crowd was drinking beer and fishing with my roommate but that was the extreme other direction as he was boring. However, he was probably the better company if I needed to make a smarter, safer choice.

Maria was older than me, she was thirty-something and I was in my early twenties. So I did learn a lot from being with her, and even our age differences as an educating experience. She taught me a lot about relationships and growing up. I give her credit for making me understand what was real in life. Therefore I applied Rule of the System #1 and appreciated her as a mentor of sorts. What I learned from her was not necessarily pleasant, but it was real. I had the first understanding after the drug deal how I was having romantic relationships the same way I was living my life—without considering consequences and the effects on others.

As the dangerous system lurked around me, I knew better but allowed myself to walk close to the line. The system—no matter whether it's the penal system, the welfare system, the military system, or the vast complexity of life systems—does plays for keeps. The rules don't bend for anyone. The system does not see color. It sees processes, and whether you are in it, around it, or aware of it will determine how the system will impact you. There are no excuses for your choices.

The initial reasons why Marie and I did not get married were because in her earlier years she was unable to have children. That was a blessing in disguise. While we did enjoy our young antics, I had no sense of values for what I wanted in relationships. She even tried to stop me from going down the wrong path with another woman, but I was still hell-bent on living my life with women with blinders on.

We attended a Fourth of July party together. At this party, there was this beautiful black woman named Heather. I'm not sure if it was jealousy of the fact I was with Marie or she truly had eyes for me, but Marie picked up on it quickly. Marie did everything she could to keep us separated and not allow any lengthy conversations to transpire between the two of us. After the party, she did make mention of this woman looking at me.

The guy who was hosting the party was a friend I met while stationed in Orlando. He was married and his wife worked with this other woman to whom I was attracted. His intentions were to set us up even though he knew I was living with Marie. Heather brought some really good food to the party in a Tupperware dish or a Pyrex dish, and when the party ended we realized Heather had left her dish at my friend's house. So, being the smooth guy I thought I was, I decided to take the dish to Heather. Heather lived about twenty-six miles away from where we were and when I brought her the dish, she was very surprised and happy. She was so impressed I went to the effort to do this that she was willing to go out to dinner with me. I was still searching for the right relationship but had not taken the time to really evaluate what kind of partner I wanted. I was young, busy, ambitious, and essentially wanted it to be easy.

That night after dinner, we talked, shared ideas about each other's family history. We agreed to see each other more. She knew I was living with Marie but she was willing to go out with me again and again. I did not implement Rule of the System #10: *Be discerning about who you trust with your ambitions.*

Marie knew I was seeing Heather and tried to warn me about her. I thought her warnings were just jealousy, but I was blinded by beauty and not by her brains, so I did not listen to Marie, and we ended up separating. We stayed friends because we worked together. She warned me it would be a huge mistake in my life if I got serious with Heather. I did not follow my own rule and trust her mentorship.

I should have thought twice about what I was doing. My ego stepped in and I thought Marie was just being jealous. I did not follow Rule of the System #4: *Never become pompous or arrogant. Adversity is not the enemy; stay humble*. I was arrogant. I was truly young and dumb. I was blinded by lust. Heather and I had discussions about her completing College. She only had three credits remaining to get her college degree, but she never went back to school. That was one telltale sign she was off-track and non-committed, but I ignored the red flag.

Heather was not a good woman, but I couldn't see it. To make matters worse, I asked Heather to marry me. I thought I could change her. Rule #7: *Never be too demanding*. Heather was this country girl who was unexposed to what I thought life had to offer. During the course of the wedding planning, Heather's friends told me they were surprised she had met such a good guy. The guy who agreed to do our photos for a wedding did it for free because he didn't believe someone was actually marrying Heather. Talk about missing signs and being blinded by lust. I did not follow Rule of the System #2 and lost my focus on the objective. I did not evaluate my game plan.

The boyfriend of Heather's mother told me I should not marry her because I was too good for her. I thought I was not too good for anyone and he was just making me feel good. I should have listened to him, but I had not dealt with my own low self-esteem.

After all, no one had told me I was important and special growing up. And the Navy wanted you to have a group mentality and look out for everyone, so I was never looking at myself. Not a lot of opportunity for self-reflection in the Navy if you don't know how to make the opportunity for change your own curriculum. I thought I at least had more things going on than she did and I could change her to be a better person, not the person others described.

Heather and I were married in December. Talk about more signs, during our wedding I had a watch on that played weird songs, and in the middle of the preacher guiding us through the vows, the song Yellow Rose of Texas started playing and I could not turn off my watch. It was somewhat hilarious but also nerve-wracking. After the ceremony, during the reception, Heather and I got into a disagreement/argument on our wedding night. It was something silly, but it was a prelude to the future. I did not see the signs. In February 1982 we received orders that would take us to Naval Air Station Bermuda.

9 ~ BERMUDA: EXPOSURE TO THE SYSTEM

My tour in Charleston came to an end and I was leaving with a new wife in tow—a wife I had only known for four months. We were off to an overseas assignment, our first duty station together in Bermuda. It was a perfect winter day with bright blue skies, warm weather, and the smell of saltwater in the air as we arrived in Bermuda. I had only ever fantasized about what this kind of tropical environment might be like. You couldn't ask for a more picturesque, pleasant day to be there. We were greeted at the airport by my sponsor. During this time in my Navy career, the Navy had a program called a sponsorship program. The sponsor's role was to greet you at the airport, get you settled into the base, and shadow you for three weeks until you were comfortable on the base. My sponsor was a guy by the name of Troy Hosmer. Troy was very cordial, kind, and grateful I was there to fill the missing gap of a duty assignment long vacant. He did exactly as planned. He ensured we received our bags and paid whatever duty we had to pay to the airport. Heading to the van, Troy asked me two very salient questions:

One: "Do you drink?"

Two: "How long have you been married?"

I told him I drank just a little and that we had only been married for one month.

Troy's response was direct.

"You'll be an alcoholic by the time you leave, and I guarantee you'll be divorced within twelve months or less."

I was shocked! What an introduction to Bermuda, but Troy had some wisdom I didn't know about at this time.

Troy was married for a handful of years. He knew what he had to deal with while stationed in Bermuda. I took his simple words of caution as just an interesting point of view that was just his opinion. I didn't understand how he could make such a judgment having never met me. Bermuda was a beautiful duty station, and my wife was a country girl who had never left the United States.

On the ride to the base, we discussed my duty assignments and how and what Heather should do while there. He mentioned she should try to get a job to keep her busy and to try to ensure that she focused on positive activities and people. It's easy to become complacent and then get involved with people or activities on the wrong side of the tracks. There's a lot about my wife I did not know, and of course how could I; I only knew her for four months. I knew she was nocturnal while I was more an early riser/early to bed person. I enjoy having intellectual conversations and she enjoyed talking about soap operas. I would ask simple questions such as what if she suddenly received $1,000,000 what would you do with it, and she would say, "I would buy me a brand new car, a house, some cool clothes. I would travel." She never once said anything stable like investing or intentions with sensibility. This went right over my head, or I chose to look the other way at these important differences. My new wife was a perfect example of what happens when you're not paying attention to what you are doing and when you allow the physical to overrule the mental aspect or love.

At this particular time in my life, I knew better. I knew the system; I knew how it worked, but I was rushed into making a very bad decision. I rushed myself. I went against everything my life experience had taught me thus far. I knew the choice I was making was wrong, but I forced the issue anyway. But this was a prime example of when you violate the rules of the system, and the system is unforgiving. I would pay dearly for this decision.

As life begin on Island, I tried to introduce my wife to the finer aspects of life. I tried to teach her how to conduct herself around senior personnel, mainly officers in the Navy. At that time I was enlisted, not really knowing I wanted to become an officer later. So, it was a privilege for me to be invited around senior personnel. She was quite the street person. Of course I came from the streets, but I was always moving away from the past. The difference being, she came from the Deep South country streets and I came from the inner-city northern streets. Two completely different experiences of the streets. On the southern streets, people told crazy stories of the past a million times. On the streets in the inner city, people plotted and planned. The streets have never done any good to anyone. I used parts of myself from the streets in the Navy, such as my ability to fight and not be scared, but Bermuda was the beginning of my life transition away from even those parts of my persona. As time progressed in Bermuda, incidents happened that caught my attention, and could no longer be overlooked.

I was gravitating toward individuals who were very positive and doing productive things in life while she was gravitating to lower species on the base. She wanted to hang out with young ladies who had five children from different men and were still single mothers. I saw no value in her having a friend of that stature since she was a married woman. My wife thought she was cool. Another sign. I'm not sure if she ever cheated on me, but my suspicion is very high that this happened. I could see it in the way she carried herself around people. She could be very flirtatious around them in my presence but play it off as just being a nice woman. Men can tell when women are advertising.

Inherent to island mentality is gossip. People spread rumors about you or about where you are or what you do just because they have nothing else better to do. Once again, my clueless wife had no idea of the scrutiny she was under. The fact that she didn't understand the importance of how you conducted yourself out in public reflected on my Navy career. I knew something was up when my co-workers would ask me about her. I would always wonder what their concern was. I'm sure they must have saw something I did not see, just like the folks back home. I was blinded by lust, or maybe now just wanted to change her because I thought she was a better person than what I saw. I wanted to make an unnatural be natural, and that simply doesn't work.

To cope with the growing suspicion and concern I had made a bad decision bringing her to Bermuda, I focused on my job and learned Rule of the System #12: *Don't let the haters distract you from your objectives.* The purpose of my assignment in Bermuda was based on my nuclear weapons background. It was critical that I strategized with the island being a contingency site for strike defense and a deterrence for attacks on the U.S. My relationship was distracting me from this critical role, and more importantly my focus on what it was going to take for me to get promoted to the next rank. I was being a homebody, studying, and making my house a home. I bought expensive top-of-the-line furniture. My pride and joy was a fascinating hidden bar. This bar looked like a nice piece of living room decor, but it opened up into a really nice bar. I had it fully stocked for guests to come over and I could offer them a beverage of their choice. Again, my idea was to accommodate the people with whom I was associating. I intended to bring class and style into my home. I put white carpet throughout the house. At the time, my sister was stationed in Germany and sent us some very beautiful German items, such as a hand-carved cuckoo clock. While I was building my future through changing my atmosphere, she was too busy gossiping in the streets and hanging out with the bad people with whom I did not want to associate. She revealed herself to be a skillful liar and a manipulator. My trust factor balanced out at zero. I was not happy in our marriage and I was sad because there was nothing I could do. We were overseas, so I could not get the marriage annulled. I had to try to work the relationship issues out.

I came home one night tired from work, happy to be walking into my beautiful home. I took my shoes off and kicked back to watch TV. She came into the house late this night. I had no idea what she had been up to. "I don't think we're going to make it," she said to me, just like that. I had no idea what that meant or where it came from.

I pondered the words she had spoken. I thought about all the different ways I tried to understand where she was coming from. And then it just came to me that all the hard work I had been doing to try to make the marriage work, she had no interest in trying to make it work. She had no interest in having a happy family. In that moment, Rule of the System #13 flooded over me: *Cut ties quickly if someone is not aligned with your vision.*

So I went in the bedroom and I gathered all her clothes and I piled them up in the living room floor.

"You can pack your s*** and go," I told her.

I realized I did not have the money to buy a plane ticket to send her home. So that night I called the airport to see how much money it would cost to get her a one-way plane ticket back to Holly Hill, South Carolina. I borrowed that exact amount from a friend and went to the airport and bought her plane ticket. I decided then and there to add Rule of the System #14: *Always have some rainy-day money.*

When I returned home, I said to her, tomorrow morning I have a t-ball game to coach. The game is from 8 a.m. to 10 a.m. Your flight is at 9 a.m.

"If you're here when I come back from my t-ball game, then it shows you're willing to work things out, but if you're not, have a nice life." I initially didn't want to accept the fact that my dream marriage was over. I was willing to try and make it work. Having now realized this was not in her plans, I needed to figure out a way to get over her.

The next day, when the game was over, I headed straight home. When I arrived, the house was empty. I didn't panic. I didn't get angry, I just said to myself, it's time to move on. I made up my mind and if she's willing to leave and not try to work things out, then it wasn't worth my time and energy. I knew then that we were not made for each other, and trying to fit a square peg into a round hole resulted in big problems. So this was a blessing in disguise. We did not have any children, so it was really more like a long one-night stand. A very expensive lesson. But I did learn, and I have no regrets.

Trust is critical when you build your life and work in all the systems around you. If I can't trust you, even to this day, I don't want to have anything to do with you. It's that simple. I don't have time. As you mature in life and the systems around you, you realize how critical the rules are and why they are. One of the key elements is understanding what trust means in the system. It could mean different things to different people, but you have to be aware of how it's being used. When you put trust on the table, it cannot be violated at all, and if it is ever violated, then it's a relationship that will never mend. Some individuals I've met along the way don't understand the rules of the system, and they let the wrong things to take priority in their life such as money or power. The system is unforgiving.

It's not hard to understand. If you will lie, cheat, and steal, then there are no limits to what you would do and I can't afford to know you. I am so glad I learned this lesson because I had to get tougher and stronger to take on the ascension in my life and the powerful people I would surround myself with.

Still, part of the education of understanding involves some regret. I was hurt and disappointed because I allowed someone to get so close to me and was violated. I took a week off from work just to think about what was going on in my life. I was twenty-one years old and very vulnerable. I spent the entire week in my house. I would get up in the morning, take a shower and then just sit and watch movies and drink. I drank a half a gallon of Johnnie Walker Red whiskey every day for five days. Surprisingly I never became drunk. I sat and watched all types of movies. I even watched the Godfather trilogy, all eight hours of it at one time. I didn't want to talk to anybody, I did not want to see anybody, I just needed to get my life together and I didn't know how. I didn't know what to do. I had never been faced with anything like this before in my life. As a young kid in high school, I had my life planned out to perfection. Now I was twenty-one years old and thought I met the love of my life because I had planned it that way. I would have the 3.2 kids and live in a house with a white picket fence no later than age of twenty-three. That was my fantasy. What this situation taught me was that's exactly what it was—a fantasy.

That week while I sat there, I had time to reflect on all the warnings I had been given about her—the guy taking photos for free at our wedding, the mother's boyfriend telling me I was too good for her, and all her friends who were shocked we were serious. I beat myself up all week about missing all of those signs. They were so clear as a bell—Stevie Wonder could have seen all these signs! My shop Chief said something to me one day that really threw me for a loop.

"I heard you have been drinking excessively."

"Have I ever came to work late?" I asked him in a somewhat smart-mouthed response.

"No," he said.

"Have my uniforms ever been improper?"

Again, he said no.

"Have I ever been late to any of my watch assignments?"

"No," he said.

"Then stay the heck out of my business," I told him.

The truth was, behind my bravado, what he had said made my insides churn. I could not sleep because I knew what he was saying was right, but I was a coward in the sense that I didn't face the challenges in front of me at that time. The good news was I was aware enough to know that if he said it to me, then obviously I have a problem. I needed to get this problem fixed right away or it would be the end of my military career. After about a week of self-punishment and tormenting, I called my mother for advice. I was thinking my mother would say to me, "Son, these are the things that happened while newlyweds and you can work things out." That was my expectation.

"Good. I hated that b**** anyway," is what my mother actually said.

I was floored to hear my mother speak those words to me, but at the same time I knew she was right. "Son, you are a good man," she said. "There are plenty of women in this world who will appreciate someone like you."

I took her words to heart and they helped me bounce back. I was through with relationships. For the time being, I had no intention on getting serious with anyone because my trust factor was totally gone.

10 ~ SPONSORING DIANE: BUILDING A LONG-LASTING PARTNERSHIP

While coaching t-ball, some of the moms knew some of the other parents were single, so of course they tried to hook me up with other single moms. They invited me out to different functions and events and I would go, but I would be a fly-on-the-wall. I had no intention of getting into a relationship with anyone. Dates were time wasters for me. Instead, I started focusing on the Masonic Lodge. I was quickly promoted to the master of the lodge and I spent all my time with my Lodge Brothers. At the time my separation occurred, there were about eight other guys who had the same thing happen to them. So, we became the separated men's club, which was somewhat hilarious. We would all sit and commiserate about what happened in our relationships. What I learned was most of us were only married for a very short time. Being on an island and married was tough. Troy had been right. Someone should have warned us prior to coming to the island how if your marriage wasn't strong you should not come. But in any case, I have no regrets or ill feelings. I learned a very valuable lesson in life from the experience. Bermuda was actually a good place for me once Heather left. I got back into the martial arts and was fighting in tournaments. I had new friends, new associations, and was truly making good changes in my life in my early twenties.

A friend told me about angels coming into my life. I never thought of it that way, but then I realized I did have a few. Back on the Dixie my angel was my Sea Daddy. In Charleston my angel was Marie. In Bermuda my angel was Troy Hosmer who indirectly planted a seed in my head about my relationship not lasting. Each one of these individuals changed my life just by being around long enough to provide me a sense of awareness I was missing at the time, but later everything they all said came to fruition. We all have a special purpose in life and have to go through experiences related to our path to see those purposes.

My upbringing in Philadelphia, the little stint I had in Georgia, the challenges I faced on the Dixie, the drug dealing on the Shenandoah, the crazy friends I met in Orlando, were all part of sorting through what was right and wrong. Now that I had learned about observing and identifying what the system is about and how events move within the system, I was preparing for change. I had learned I couldn't fake my way through the system. I understood and accepted it was real. It was that simple.

I had no idea how big that change would be, but it was coming and fast. You can't force the change, you can only desire it and then you have to let life take you down that path. My change came in Bermuda when I unexpectedly met my best friend. Like Troy had been assigned to be my sponsor, I was assigned to be Diane Boston's sponsor. The last thing I wanted to do was be responsible for a woman after my failed marriage, but I was a good sailor and I did what I was told. I went to the airport to meet Diane. When I first saw Diane, I said welcome to Bermuda. I asked her a little bit about herself and she told me where she was from. She was somewhat of a shy girl. I took my job seriously and let her know I would be there for her. I made sure I showed her around the island properly, got her settled into the barracks, and got her settled into the shop. I hung around until she was stable on the base. The more I hung around Diane, the more she kind of grew on me. interestingly enough, I saw other guys looking at her, and I felt very protective of her. So I shooed them away. I was a pretty mean dude back then and I had a lot of respect from the men on the base, so the last thing they wanted to do was tangle with me. We started to spend lots of time together outside the scope of the Navy. We would ride my motorcycle and she would come to my martial arts tournaments. We went out to concerts together. It was awesome hanging out with her.

After about six months, I finally realized I had deep feelings for Diane I thought I would never have for anyone else again. At six months I kissed her and told her what I thought of her. That was the beginning of the serious change. We would go out partying and I wouldn't have to drink, and she would stick by my side and not let anyone bother me. We became inseparable. We worked in the same shop together, so we went to lunch together. One of our mutual friends eventually said, I bet you guys are going to get married.

"No chance in heck," was my reply. We were best friends and that's all I thought I we would ever be.

One of the funniest moments we had together was after we had been hanging out for over six months or so. I asked to take her out to dinner. I took her to one of the fanciest restaurants on the island. A that time, spending $75 per plate was considered a very expensive restaurant for Bermuda. We had a very delightful evening and when the meal was over, I gave her a kiss on the cheek and took her home. Years later, deep into our marriage, I learned she wrote home to her mother that night and told her about me, the beautiful restaurant, and that she almost felt obligated to do something with me, but didn't. She told her mother I was a nice guy and my family had a farm in Georgia. Her mother wrote her back and said good, you didn't owe him anything, don't trust him, he probably owns swampland in Georgia, and because he's in the Masonic lodge he's a no-good guy! To this day, we still chuckle about her mom's response!

I had to overcome issues I went through with my divorce. I needed to realize how all women are not bad, conniving, and sneaky. Although some of the women in my life at this particular time appeared to have a particular agenda, I didn't realize until later that not all are cut from the same cloth. You have to be very careful about stereotyping. You can't base all your decisions on a particular circumstance you're in. One person or two may operate similarly, but it doesn't categorically mean everyone is the same. It is imperative you practice daily discernment to see what's real and what's not. Then you will realize how all people are not the same.

Diane was a compassionate, very understanding, beautiful soul. One evening, we were on the motorcycle heading to dinner to meet friends. We were driving in the rain, and came upon a very sharp curve. I was trying to negotiate this turn and my front wheel lost traction. I was horrified because I had Diane on the back of the bike and if I did not regain control of the bike we would go over a cliff of about 150 feet into shoal rocks. There's no way we would have survived such an accident. I did everything in my power to keep that motorcycle on two wheels and regain traction on the front wheel. We made it around the turn safely. Later at the restaurant, Diane scolded me. "Maxwell, you should not play around when we riding a motorcycle in the rain."

She had no idea how close her life was to a tragic ending. I never told Diane the real story until months later. But we decided if we were going to go out on dates together, we needed to buy a car. Our first car together was a Chrysler Avenger. It was an English car, so the steering wheel was on the wrong side and it was a stick shift, which Diane had no idea how to drive. So there we were with a manual transmission alone a steering wheel on the wrong side. What is most important here to note is we were working as a team. I had come to realize how imperative it was to have a good teammate. In order for you to be a good teammate, you both have to have the same objectives as the relationship starts growing. You cannot wait until after you are married to decide whether or not this is the right person for you. You have to identify all these criteria early on in the relationship. So, becoming best friends makes the process natural. It cannot be forced. Some of the fallacies in the system arise when people try to force situations because this doesn't work if it's not natural. You must do this with your eyes wide open. You cannot make exceptions when you're looking for a natural solution. It is critical that when you mitigate an exception, you can truly live it with for a long time.

As best friends, we respectfully put our money in together to buy a car so we were safe. As our relationship developed, we decided to open up a checking account together. The checking account was in both our names and it took both signatures to cash a check. Instead of spending money out of each other's pocket, we would each deposit a certain amount of money each payday so when we went to go hang out together, we would spend from our combined savings in our checking account. That actually worked out very well. We bought a stereo and a VCR.

What I began to learn about Bermuda was how it was a very enchanting Island as long as you're with the right person. I did not let the outside influences affect the relationship. I had a vision of happiness and had thoughts of working together to accomplish goals. I learned in my previous relationships what is not compatible you have to change immediately. You have to have the internal fortitude to make the change. You also cannot force something that's not meant to be. You can't settle for what you've got if it's not the right thing. All too often in life we are faced with decisions that could be life-changing but we just accept the way the times are because we're afraid to change. This is the worst mistake anyone can ever make. In Bermuda I started learning about the woman of my dreams She was wise, beautiful, and intelligent—she had everything I could dream up.

I finally took the plunge for marriage. We already acted like we were married. I said that to her. That was my proposal. She said yes. When we decided to get married, Diane was still of an age where she needed to have her parent's permission. Her mother had turned over a new leaf and accepted me—not liked me, just accepted me. There is a difference! Her parents agreed and signed for her to get married. Since we both were in the military, we had to go through counseling with the military chaplain. At first I was dead set against this because I saw no value. I thought he would just ask me a bunch of humdrum, mundane, ridiculous questions. I was surprised by the questions he asked me about her family, like how did her brother squeeze the toothpaste from the toothpaste tube, and what upset her mother. What were her sister's favorite things in life. He asked me very few questions about Diane. The beauty of this approach was so often people marry someone not realizing they are marrying the family too. In this process, I got to learn a little bit more about Diane's family. I learned how our families had a lot in common.

No Yellow Rose of Texas playing in the background, no arguing at the ceremony. We had a very simple wedding. It was only me, Diane, her bridesmaid and my groomsman, the preacher, and her friend in the audience. That was the grand total at the ceremony. For our reception, you had to pay for your meal but we had an open bar. We had a very nice crowd that participated in our wedding. Our wedding bliss and joy we shared on our honeymoon was straight out of a Harlequin novel. Thirty-five years later, it's still the same. Diane has been the biggest angel in my life. We had a very good time on that little Island in the Atlantic Ocean. During our honeymoon, we found out we had made the promotion board and we were pregnant.

Having Diane in my life helped me appreciate all the angels that were around me, but most importantly I appreciated the ability to recognize what the Angels were saying to me.

If you know you are strong in one area, but weak in another, focus on your weakness. You have to be real and honest with yourself. If you are truly weak in an area, it doesn't matter what the area is; it could be in high-level thinking or simple math problems. Whatever it is, you have to be able to accept the fact you're weak in that area. It's okay to be weak in certain areas because you have two choices: Either you build up in that area or you rely on your newfound partner to have strengths in areas where you are weak. This is where having a good partner comes into play because you need to have someone you truly trust who will give you an unbiased account. They are not afraid to show you areas where you are weak, and help you get stronger.

I don't need to spend time learning more about my strengths, but rather master the areas where I am less proficient. Put your energy on your weaknesses and not on your strengths because you've already mastered your strengths but you haven't mastered your weaknesses. Learn how to overcome your shortcomings if you want to become a whole person.

After we were married, we were coming up on change of station orders. Because we both were in the military at the time, we were trying to get placed at the same Duty station. It did not look too promising for us. Back then, the Navy was not concerned about keeping families together, but rather filling the spots for needs of the Navy. They were going to send one of us to Yorktown, Virginia and the other one was going to a school and after school who knows. Diane and I had to sit down and talk about our future. The decision now that we were pregnant and could potentially be stationed at two different duty stations was how would we manage and raise children in a military family separately.

Back then in the 1980s, the Navy's policy was when a woman was in her fifth trimester, they gave her an option to get out of the Navy with an honorable discharge. Diane and I discussed this and we decided one of us needed to get out of the Navy. Having an intellectual conversation with someone is far better than arguing and being stupid, so we weighed our options. I was being promoted to E6 and Diane was being promoted to E4. I had been in the Navy for about six years and Diane had only been in for two. Logically looking at this decision, it made more sense for Diane to get out and follow my career than for me to get out and follow her career. We chose together that Diane would get out and follow my career. Instead of trying to decide which duty station would be next, we ended up going to Orlando for me to attend the Advanced Torpedo Technical school called Mark 540. It was by far one of the hardest and toughest torpedoman mate advanced technical schools the rating had to offer.

My three-year tour in Bermuda was equivalent to a Harvard doctoral degree in life. I learned so much about people and weathering change. I learned about wisdom and how to operate in an unknown environment. The benefit of the system is that if you understand where you are at, you can navigate that new system to help operations in an unknown environment. Don't let this scare you; this situation is positive because now you have to trust your judgment and you have to trust your instincts. You can use your own Rules of the System to grow and change from any experience, or implement mine. Wisdom comes from listening to older people or people who have experience you're trying to gain. Wisdom is not about judging or Monday morning quarterbacking how you could have done something different than someone else. Wisdom is listening to what's being said and then understanding why it was said.

11 ~ BACK TO ORLANDO

Orlando, Florida in 1985 was quite the place to be. It was very humid with torrential downpours at three o'clock p.m. in the afternoon. Droves of ladybugs flew in the air, clogging up your car radiator. You had to buy a bug screen and put it on the front of your car. Diane was pregnant with our first child, and we had very little money coming in at this time. We got very creative with ways to have fun on the cheap. The classes I attended were some of the toughest classes the Navy had to offer. With Diane being pregnant and the classes being so tough, even with all of that stress I somehow managed to make it through.

We were thankful I had a cousin who lived in Cocoa Beach, Florida, which was only about an hour away. The cost to go there was minimal. We would visit them on the weekends. After we paid all of our bills, we would only have about $20 to spend until the next pay period. My cousin, who was a retired army guy, would always give me a hard time about joining the Navy. He felt we were an Army family. But whenever we went to visit them, we never had to spend any money. My cousins would always ensure we had the best time of our lives for that weekend. They would always barbecue and take us to different venues. They treated us right. What they didn't know was we had no money and of the $20 we had, $10 of it went into gas to get back and forth to Cocoa Beach.

We never focused on money. Diane and I always had such a great time just being together. Our standard weekend schedule was on Friday nights we would watch wrestling, on Saturdays channel 35 would show old war movies. The theme was "TV 35 goes to War." On Sundays we would play two-player board games at home. We had a very small one-bedroom apartment, but it worked well with just the two of us, and after the baby was born, the crib didn't take up much room.

If we wanted to see a movie at the theater, we would follow the new movie circuit as the movie played in the various movie theaters and when it reached the 99-cent theater, then we would go and see whatever movie was playing. I also didn't have enough money to drink a lot; I would buy one Schlitz Malt Liquor bull beer. I would buy this type of beer because of its potency and drinking it slow or little at a time to last a week. On our way to the Lamaze classes, we also enjoyed going to 7-Eleven and buying Slurpees. We were so satisfied with our life we didn't worry about not having any money.

The lesson here is to marry someone you can enjoy time with regardless of your income level. Looking at relationships in this system, it's critical to understand your potential life partner is also part of your system. The two of you need to leverage knowledge to ensure the path you're on is the same. My lovely bride and I have been married for over thirty-five years and we have never had one argument. The reason why we haven't had an argument is because we enjoy being around each other, we respect each other, and we know that working the system together we can quickly accomplish much more when we're side-by-side than when we're in strife. Most people I know with failed marriages never became friends first or started out with the same objectives. They both had individual agendas that at some point collided. So it's important you know up front who your potential life partner is because this could be the determination of making or breaking how you travel through life and the systems of life.

I never looked back or had any regrets for choosing my Diane.

Our first set of furniture we bought was from the Montgomery Ward store, and we charged it on our charge card we had just received. Before that, for furnishing our apartment, we did the rent-to-own routine. We were preparing for three of my nieces to visit us, so we needed someplace for them to sit. Being a good uncle and aunt, we took them to Disney World when they visited, as all three of them were very young. Having limited funds, the way we were able to get Disney World tickets was funny. We would sit through a 90-minute timeshare presentation where the tickets were promised at the end. We would, of course, say no to the great deal they offered. Before heading over to the presentation, we would practice saying no despite the pressure that was put on us about purchasing a timeshare. The answer was always no, then we would get the prize and leave. Diane was and is truly my soulmate.

We also had to buy a new car with no money. Florida was just as racist as Georgia. Because we were a young black couple, the car dealers would offer us cars that were the stereotypical vehicles most blacks would drive. Diane and I were at the car dealership, she looking like she's about to pop any minute, and this guy wants to sell us a two-seater 240Z. I looked at this guy and asked him was he just stupid or didn't know better. Sadly, he still tried to convince me that it was the right car for my new family and me. We knew it was time to leave this dealership; there was no sense in talking to someone so stupid. The guy even suggested we could put a baby seat in the back of this little car. The next dealer was offering us another car we could not afford; we did not buy that car. I went to another dealership to purchase a car, and this guy sold us a lemon that wouldn't accelerate past twenty miles an hour. Suddenly that was my problem and not the car's problem. After a very stern discussion with him, he gave us yet another car, which was also a piece of junk. Two months later, and exchanging five cars, we finally found the right car. While we were closing the deal, the financial lady at the counter told me I had to pay an additional four dollars for the auto transfer fee. At this point, I was so frustrated and angry at this dealership, I said to her I would not give her one extra dime. I made such a scene over this, but Diane said, "Honey, I'll pay the four dollars." "No, you will not," I said, fuming.

The lady behind the counter said she would pay the additional four dollars. I think she was trying to de-escalate the scene because she was worried things were getting out of hand over four dollars. I firmly said, "I don't care who pays it, but I'm not paying it."

I did not pay the four dollars, and I did get the car. The car was very nice, and it lasted us quite some time. The moral of this story is you must fight for what you think is right. My issue wasn't with the four dollars. My issue was with the car dealership not being honorable and trying to sell my pregnant Diane and me a car they knew was not suitable for us. They didn't care what it did for my family and me. So to stand up to them despite the challenges was the right thing to do in my mind, and this taught me another aspect of navigating life. There will be times when you're traveling through life and the various systems you'll be up against will force you to take a stance on a principle and you can't be afraid to do that. It's not about win or lose. It's about right and wrong when it comes to a principle. If you're a person with a passive personality, I can almost guarantee you will live a miserable life. The system is unforgivable, and if you don't control the system, it can and will control you.

Our beautiful first child, a daughter, was born July 25, 1985. I was still in school, and the Navy was not playing games. The schoolwork was hard. I would come home from school after twelve-hour days, and Diane would ask me to take over baby duties. I never said no, but sometimes I would be so tired it felt like I had sand in my eyes. I would take my little baby girl and put her on my chest, and we would lay on the couch and sleep. Diane would fuss at me about potentially dropping the baby, but that never happened. It was very interesting to know I could be in a deep sleep and have my baby on my chest, and she was a part of me. I never dropped her, and we always had a very peaceful time sleeping together. The three of us would still go down to Cocoa Beach to visit family, but less frequently because now we had to buy diapers. We still did the Friday night wrestling, the Saturday TV 35, and the Sunday games. We were truly off to a great start in our marriage and our relationship, and most importantly, our friendship.

One night while sitting at home in Orlando, there was a knock on our door. We were somewhat shocked because we didn't know anyone there locally, so why someone would come to visit us in Orlando so late in the evening. Because this was late evening, it was kind of scary, and I did not have any weapons in the house to protect us. I opened the door carefully, and to our surprise, it was an old friend from Bermuda who tracked us down and came to visit. He was from Hollywood, Florida, which is in South Florida. This guy was a very interesting character. He's the only guy I knew who the Navy allowed to use drugs and did not kick him out. When he failed a urine test, he told the navy he was addicted to pot. They told him that every time he was given a urine test, it had to be positive or they would kick him out for lying. He was a funny guy because when he stuttered, he slapped his forehead. So imagine someone talking to you, constantly pounding their forehead. It was quite hilarious. At the time of his visit, he was either in transition out of the Navy or being assigned a new duty station, presumably because of his drug use.

He was certainly part of the old me, not part of the new me. I was kind to him, and we drank a beer, and then he took off. He was a reminder of the type of people Diane and I did not want to socialize with moving forward. If he had moved to Orlando, I'm sure we would not have hung out together. This was a typical Navy connection. He was more of a duty station friend, not a long-term friend. I appreciate him coming back into my life for that blip of time to solidify the lesson for me. After that night, we never heard from him again.

There are times while we're traveling through the systems of life we are reminded of the people who have come in and out. It's important to understand not everybody who comes into your life is there to be your friend. They may be there just to show you something about yourself or give you a glimpse of your future. You have to be smart enough to know whether to hold on or to let go. There is an old adage out there that says people come into your life for a season, a reason, or a lifetime, and you have to be able to discern which one it is.

The Advanced Torpedo Technical school class series had a fifty-percent attrition rate. Only myself and a fellow sailor name Dave Munoz completed it out of the four of us. Dave had a learning disability as it related to technical stuff, so getting through these classes was tough, and he barely made it through all of the schools. I helped him prepare for the advanced technology classes and the toughest parts of the curriculum. When it came down to the last portion of this long process, I asked Dave to assist me, and he turned his back on me. Also, when we were doing our final practical exam, Dave was what we called in the Navy a brown-noser. The teachers favored Dave and gave him a softball for his final practical problem. Based on the teacher's help, obviously, he completed his assignment quickly. When it was my turn, I received a much tougher practical test, and during my troubleshooting, I asked Dave for assistance.

"I'm not helping you because I won't be with you out in the fleet, so figure it out yourself," said Dave.

While that irked me to no end, but what Dave thought hurt me actually helped me. Dave's reaction caused me to do some self-reflecting to know he was right, that I have to press on without people like him. This made me a stronger and more determined individual. Dave's career ended after this class. He never was promoted again, whereas I went on to get promoted as an officer.

A very valuable lesson I learned is that when you help people, you cannot expect anything in return. Just like when you loan money, don't expect to get it back. In this particular situation, I thought this person was a good guy so I went above and beyond to help him. At the end of the day, all this person saw was an opportunity to use me to get what he wanted. But there's another old adage that says he who laughs first, laughs last. Dave's actions, although they bothered me, were countered by knowing when his career ended right there at the E6 level while I went into the officers corps. So who had the last laugh?

The one beautiful thing about the system is that once you navigate with the rules you have learned through trial and error, then it becomes very easy to live your life. Again, another lesson here: Be careful who you help. Not all people have good intentions. Sometimes wolves are in sheep's clothing. People who appear to mean good, or who you help, may have no good intentions for you. They are just riding along as a user. That's who Dave was. I am glad I had that lesson because I have a sharper radar for users now.

When you run across someone who you know does not have good intentions and you still try to help them, don't expect a good ending.

My life was progressing smoothly and I found out I would be assigned to the Philippines as my next duty station, and now instead of going solo, I would be going with Diane and a baby. Life got fuller, richer, and more complicated, so maturing faster was in order. Why? The Philippines was known for causing most marriages to fail.

12 ~ THE PHILIPPINES: ESTABLISHING A MORAL CODE

When we arrived in the Philippines, it was over one hundred degrees on a December evening after a long international flight. I was in my heavy winter dress blues. By the time I got off the plane and walked to the airport terminal door, I was soaking wet. The humidity was at least 100%. Welcome to the PI (short for the Philippines). The Philippines was a whole different world that was going to test every moral fiber of my being: Humanity, loyalty, dedication, and most of all, my marriage.

Travelers and tourists experience the vacation version of the Philippines, but I was about to take on the military version. In places like the PI, sin is a joke, and the wild adult antics people talk about are the reality. There were a lot of long-term marriages destroyed, and a lot of new marriages began, but only to the PI girls who just wanted a free ticket to the U.S. So as a new father, dad, husband, and friend coming to a place like this made me scrutinize my morality meter.

My first day after getting Diane and my daughter settled in at the Navy Lodge, my military sponsors came to my room and told me because I was new, it was customary that we go out. My wife was kind enough to allow me to do that. Being a former military person, she understood the customs and traditions. She was exhausted from the eighteen-hour flight and jet lag. She was also dealing with our six-month-old baby girl. The PI is a poor third-world country, and the Navy base was the center of economic support for that local area in the Philippines. During the normal times when the fleet was out, the U.S. base spent approximately two or three million dollars a night. When the fleet pulled into port, the sailors spent ten to thirteen million dollars a night!

The town only existed because of the military base. During the day, you had the normal events that took place like local vendors on the side of the streets. But the nightlife got exciting and crazy, especially when battlegroups came into port and sailors had a lot of money burning in their pockets to spend. Because I was stationed there, I was quickly titled as a "station ditto." This term was used to identify people who were stationed there for a three-year tour or longer. The locals knew if you were a regular as they would see you more often as opposed to when the ships came in. They capitalized on the sailors who were in port for a few nights.

In most cases when you were a station ditto, you were able to do business differently. You could negotiate for long-term deals because they knew they would see you again. Filipinos have an incredible memory. If you ever touch foot on that soil and someone there knew you, and they were there when you came back, they did not forget you.

We would go out to a club that was supposed to be the Torpedo shop crew's favorite place to go. Most of the clubs were like gentlemen's clubs. They were not like your normal discotheque. A woman comes up to you and asks you to buy her a drink. If you say yes, then she becomes your evening's entertainment. For some of the guys who found this appealing, they can take that to the next level and pay what they call her "bar fine." You pay the owner of the bar a certain amount of money, and you could take this lady out of the bar, and she stays with you all night long. As an American, you were seen as the financial entity to support the local economy. You had to be mindful of how you conducted yourself at all times. Bottom line, you were an ambassador of the United States of America.

I didn't know how to handle myself with all the shenanigans going on around me and I didn't stay very long. I was thinking about Rule of the System #8: *Be flexible to change but stand your ground ethically.* We went out to other bars and walked up and down the streets seeing sailors acting foolishly and young ladies trying to get them to come into their clubs. The drink of choice was San Miguel beer. This beer did not have any quality control standard, so you could drink one beer and it would have no effects and then drink the second one and someone would have to carry you home.

Living in the Philippines you quickly established an understanding of what was real and what was fantasy. It was very easy to get caught up in the party girls and the bar events. Your long-term focus should have been your family relationship (if you were married with kids) when your tour was over; you would go back home, hopefully with the wife you went over there with initially. The military experience was very strict about adultery and what the girl's ploy was out in the town, only because they were well-trained and eager to get a free ride to the U.S. The young ladies knew what to say and do to distract you out in town. When I talk about morality, it is easy to cheat or party too much without anyone knowing or finding out. This was a normal routine out on the street. It was important to understand how in this environment, you had to know the definition of integrity, of doing what is right when no one is looking.

I cannot say this enough…the system is unforgiving. So if you understand this concept then you must understand you have to do the right thing when no one is looking. Because that's going to determine in most cases the difference between success or failure and what's truly in your heart. Integrity is just that, doing the right thing when no one is looking because that behavior shapes your character. Your character defines who you are and it also defines how you will operate within the system.

One of the shop rules in the Philippines was when we had a new person, because of the distractions out in the town, for the first month no work was assigned to them. Acclimating yourself to the surrounding environment can take at least a month, meaning a lot of partying a lot of drinking; your head is out in the streets going to gentlemen's clubs, and this was not just only for men. This craziness was for women as well. This was a whole new environment from the United States Navy. So shortly after arriving, I was introduced to a gentleman by the name of Larry. Larry told me he was going to take me under his wing and show me the ropes. Larry was a little younger than I, so as it worked out. He mentored me about the location, and I mentored him about the Navy. Larry said, let's go to Subic City.

We get in a Jitney, which is a Filipino means of transportation like an open bus or jeep. On the ride, you're in the mix with locals, and typically you're the only one or two Americans on board, so first of all, the price for the locals is much lower than it is for you the American. The Jitney ride was through Olongapo City, through the Barrio and then to Subic City. In the Barrio, there is nothing but bars and bars and bars. We stopped there briefly to have a few beers and get primed with alcohol before getting to Subic, which I learned was a super-crazy place real fast. We had not been to Subic City for more than a minute, and all the girls in the street start running up screaming Larry, Larry, Larry! Larry was young and single and was well-known in Subic.

Larry commences to give the girls money and candy or whatever it was he was doing while I sat back thinking, what the heck is going on here. Larry took me to his favorite bar called Tramppers, one of the better of the bunch. If you bought the girls in the bar a gallon of Ube ice cream and introduced yourself to the bar owner, you could sit in the bar without being accosted by the women. The ladies in this no-holds-barred club would do what they called a peso show. The women would stack pesos on a bottle and then sit down on the bottle and pick up the pesos with her private parts. She would then release them one at a time, three at a time, two at a time. It was unbelievable. They would sit on boiled eggs and shoot them across the room. They would smoke cigarettes with their private parts. Seeing is believing in these instances because if someone had told me about it second-hand, I would have only imagined half the insanity since I had no frame of reference. Welcome to the Philippines. Now you can understand why you did not assign new sailors any task for at least for the first month of their arrival to the Philippines. You had to let them get this out of their system. I was an exception, not so much because I had a kid and was married, but because I loved them dearly enough not to do anything that would compromise my standing in my family. I did not let the craziness affect me. I focused my energies on work and understanding this new system.

Working in the system, you have to keep your apertures open at all times because the system is forever changing as your environment changes. You have to be aware of the changes around you because like I spoke of earlier, you set your goals with the end in mind, and sometimes the system will shift on you. So you have to be able to shift with it while keeping your rules and intentions top of mind. Your intended goal may change on you, but that's okay because as long as you aim high, you will hit high. Be ready at all times while operating in the system and be open to change.

That evening was an eye-opener of what was in store for the next three years while living in the Philippines. I had to make a conscious decision of what was important in my life, and that was my wife, my child, and my job. I shared with Diane the incredible things I witnessed. When you and your soulmate can engage in open communication, it's very helpful in challenging times. I knew where my military career was heading, and I couldn't afford to let what was going on outside those gates affect my future. I established my last and final Rule of the System, #15: *In marriage, effective communication is paramount.* With the strength of our marriage, I focused on getting to know the movers and the shakers on the base and left the shenanigans for the fools.

History was about to be made in the Philippines, and we were in the midst of the turmoil. Initially, we were assigned housing in a little town called San Miguel approximately 1 an hour-and-a-half away from Subic City, which was my real assigned duty station, so I had to commute back and forth to work daily. In February of 1986, the president of the Philippines, Marcos, was ousted out of the country. With the ousting of the President, the Navy made me leave my family in San Miguel and go to my assigned duty in Subic City. Diane and my eighteenth-month-old daughter Daphane were alone to fend for themselves. My wife and I had great communications, and we had direct deposit, so she had access to money. Other military members did not, and this was in the mid-1980s before the direct deposit was required. Diane and I, since we had established ourselves as such a team before we made this voyage together, were a lot smarter than most. During this time, the military was transitioning from paper checks to direct deposit. Eventually, Diane was a mentor and leader for a lot of the other wives who had husbands who did not have direct deposit. Without direct deposit, they had no means of getting money on payday. The day after the ousting, we were taking our normal route home through Olongapo City for drinks. We would stop in the Barrio and do the usual drinking or hit several bars, and lastly we would stop in a little town called San Antonio before reaching home. This particular night when I arrived home a little tipsy, Diane was hysterical, and I had no idea what was going on. She thought something had happened to me because of what was going on in the news. Unbeknownst to us when we left the base, the locals were rioting and had turned an ambulance over in the streets, blocking the base we were just in..

So when we arrived on the base at San Miguel, the locals placed a telephone pole across the streets, blocking the base entrance. I had no idea this was happening and felt irresponsible even though we didn't have cell phones back then.

I had a solid family relationship, and a good career going, and I was able to adjust to a new temporary assignment just fine. For three weeks I had to be separated from my family in a foreign country. I could have sat and drank for the time I was separated from my family, but instead I focused my energy on doing a great job at work. We were responsible for building weapons for ships heading to the Persian Gulf; I saw an opportunity to advance; therefore, I took charge of what I was tasked to do in the shop as the Leading Petty Officer. The role of the Leading Petty Officer is to lead and guide the E6 and below. I guided those junior sailors in their daily work assignments within the weapons shop and coordinated with the seniors enlisted E7 and above and the officers to ensure we were doing what we had orders to do.

13 ~ The ASROC Shop: Learning the Criticality of the System

I was a very junior E6 Petty Officer, brand new in the shop. I had only been assigned for about six or seven months. Based on the long schooling I just completed in Orlando, I was assigned to the weapons buildup and teardown section. I was also assigned to the ASROC shop. Both areas were outside of the training I had just received. I did not complain, I just worked hard to improve the shop's overall productivity and identify different areas I wanted to work at or work in at that time. My leadership there saw my drive and tenacity. My Leadership decided to promote me to the two areas of the weapons shop I wanted to be in charge of. The two shops were the MK540 computer shop and the Torpedo Record Management System (TRMS) shop, and I was trained in both areas. I quickly established myself as one of the go-to guys in the shop and before I knew it, my performance in the shop and commitment to the job was superior to my peers, so I was selected over seventeen other individuals who were senior to me to become the shop's Leading Petty Officer. Making a move like that upsets the apple cart, and I had some individuals who said they refused to work with someone Junior to them. I needed to incorporate a whole new style of leadership and management to overcome a senior E6 Petty Officer who didn't want to work for me.

When you're operating in the system, you will be tested to see just how well you understand your surroundings. Again, constantly survey the environment to ensure every day you see where you are at. This is your defining moment as to whether you have truly graduated to understanding life is a system or whether you are just faking your way through it. The system has a way of flushing out honorable people. I knew I personally couldn't resolve the issues so I had to reach out for resources more powerful than my adversary in order to win. I had to be smart enough to know not to go head-to-head but to seek additional support from my senior leadership Division Officer and department head-level staff. And that's what I did.

So this is where you take your pride and stick it in your pocket and use your moral compass in judgment and character to do the right thing to stand up for what's right and to get the right results you're seeking. But you can never let someone bulldoze you while you're operating in the system.

I contrast two men here; Larry, who was a crazy young guy but he had a good head on his shoulders, and Dale Johnson, a big guy from the South who had a deep voice everyone loved, except for my wife Diane. Diane is very easygoing. She gets along with almost everyone, yet there was something about him that rubbed her the wrong way. He was the first person I've ever seen Diane tell to his face she did not like him and did not approve of him being around me. I did not see the harm. I selected Larry to be my shop supervisor because we were very similar in our thought process. He was extremely junior to a whole bunch of people. Larry was only an E5 filling an E6 position. My seniors allowed me to make the decision to put Larry in that position and our friendship grew even closer. Larry was from Texas, and the Navy was his saving grace as it was mine. We often talked about our upbringing and how we felt we were blessed to overcome that situation.

One day we would both get selected to be officers in the United States Navy with commissioning dates very close to each other, so we were able to get commissioned simultaneously. Once you understand the direction in which you're headed, surround yourself with like-minded people who appreciate what your possibilities are. The reason for this is that they will understand your rationale for your decisions, as opposed to having to explain on various levels why you're doing what you're doing. Identify people who understand how to operate in the same system you're operating in. Or at least be around people who understand how the system operates. Together, you can achieve great success.

Johnson was a different story. Like Larry, he asked me to go out with him one night. I knew quickly the night we were out that situations were getting out of hand. I asked him to bring me home. He was drunk while he was driving and ran into a local's vehicle. Knowing I could be implicated, I wanted to get to a safe place (home) without being connected to him. He said a couple of curse words and all we have to do is get on base, and there's nothing they could do to us. He was right. Back then, you had the standard forces of agreement in place there for other countries and could not prosecute American citizens. We arrived at my house, and I knew the condition Johnson was in, and I tried to convince him not to go back out until he sobered up. He had gotten away with a crime—a hit-and-run—yet he was going to go back out to tempt his fate. I tried to take his keys, but he wouldn't listen. He was just hard-headed and determined. He went back out by himself that night, and I stayed home with my wife and child. His wife called my house and asked Diane if we were together. Diane told her no, that I was home where I belonged (the perfect alibi).

The next morning at about 6:30 a.m. I get a phone call from Johnson asking me to come and get him out of jail because he had got caught that night for drinking and driving out in town and for a charge of hit-and-run. As I had planned, I made the right decision leaving him to his own devices and not going back out in town with him that night.

Johnson was one of the many Petty Officers who were senior to me but also worked for me; I had to go out and get him and bring him back to the shop to plead his case to the seniors. I turned over the case to my boss, and we had a meeting about Johnson. My department head was this tall skinny redheaded guy who was as weird as weird can get. Most of us Junior personnel had little or no respect for him, but he was the boss. His name was Lieutenant Commander Villanova; I'm not sure what rock this guy crawled out from under, but he was a whole different breed. You never wanted to get cross-threaded or on his bad side. He did not have a sense of humor, nor did he have great people skills. Villanova took what Johnson did personally. He brought the Division Officers, the leading Chiefs, and myself in a room together and said he was going to make an example out of Johnson as what *not* to do with your Navy career.

Because I was Johnson's first-line supervisor, I had to write his evaluations with my recommendations on what to do with him. Johnson was my friend, and I was with him the night of this incident, but no one in the chain of command knew it. Johnson didn't know how connected I was with upper leadership. In some cases, when you're operating within the system, you can't share with people close to you how you understand the various systems around you. You might be operating in a higher level of thinking and have to deal with your so-called friend or acquaintance that's still lingering in old lessons without any progression. You have to be able to operate without disclosing your abilities and what you're capable of while dealing with in these situations. In some cases when confronted, you don't lie to people; you just don't tell him the whole truth. Always think ahead for a way out of situations. Or never put yourself in a situation you can't get out of successfully. Moving about in the system is a strategy game where you have to be thinking all the time.

In our meeting with senior leadership about Johnson, I was specifically told how to write Johnson's evaluations. I tried to give him fair marks so that Mr. Villanova did not recommend discharging him out of the Navy. When I submitted my first set of evaluations, I was called into the office, and I was told to mark Johnson very harshly and not to give him a mark over 3.4. I should not highlight any of Johnson's accomplishments, only focus on the negatives. I felt horrible being in that position, but this was my first time truly understanding leadership. I repeat over and over in this book: The system is unforgiving. As you navigate through the various levels of the system, you have to tuck your emotions deep inside of you and not let them show.

In this particular case, I knew the story and its ending, but I could not disclose it to the person I was close to who challenged the system. He didn't understand how the system can chew you up and spit you out. As a matter of fact, I was a part of the blades that sliced him into pieces. You still have to sleep at night despite decisions you make in leadership positions, and you will as long as you're making decisions for the right reasons and you're not controlling a situation someone else created that's against the system.

While in the middle of this process, I went to my Division Officer Mr. Anthony Rin, a young new Ensign who had only been a commissioned officer for approximately one year. He was a guy that slipped through the cracks; he had no business being an officer. He had no leadership skills one could glean knowledge from at any time. He would sit in his office and shine his rank insignia. He was more interested in trying to date Mr. Villanova's secretary than he was about his military career. Because he was a brand-new Limited Duty Officer (LDO), he didn't have any real experience with leading a shop as big as the one to which we were assigned. Therefore he had no idea what he was doing. The only reason I went to him was that in the military pecking order, he was my Division Officer. My first in command of the officer's ranks.

Despite my lack of respect for him, I had no choice but to go to him for advice. This was the system of the Navy. The system is a process and the mission is to not let yourself get caught up in personal feelings toward someone even if you don't respect them. You still have to find their use in your system. Everyone has value at some point in time.

I was tormented about this Johnson thing and needed to seek some advice on what was going on inside me. I went to Mr. Rin and asked: "Who gives me the right to control someone's pay, someone's livelihood, and someone's family?" I was expecting some long dissertation about life and all this other stuff, because Mr. Rin enjoyed pontificating about nothing important, but his answer was surprisingly simple.

"This is leadership."

Instead of him stepping up to the plate as his Division Officer and taking care of his people and helping out Johnson, he just let the bus run right over him.

Truth: The naval system doesn't care about the people; it cares about the mission. The Navy is not about emotions and feelings. The Navy expects you to know the system and understand how it's laid out to effectively maneuver in it. if you spend your time trying to worry about people and their thoughts or how they operate in the system, you will be wasting your time and energy, so stay focused. The Navy is a good example of the military system in general says we need a body that can do x, y, and z. It doesn't care who that body is. It just cares that a body has the qualifications, and if that body gets destroyed or killed in the process, they erase the number and put a new number in the slot. This is a good lesson to learn because sometimes we get caught up in how good we are or how many ribbons or awards we have. None of those accolades matter to the system. The system cares about you filling a slot. This is a very humbling awareness, but it's good to know so you don't get things twisted when you think you're all that and a bag of chips.

Proceeding forward through the system as a number in a slot was a big punch in the gut of reality for me, but I understood it as it related to dealing with Johnson. As I wrote Johnson's evaluations, I had to be honest about his professional conduct or the lack thereof, and talk about what he did and about his shortcomings. Diane and I were reflecting on how easily something like this can happen to anyone and how one person controlled your career. When I turned in my second set of evaluations, they were horrible but were approved. Mr. Villanova then had the entire shop out front and in ranks as he proceeded to tell us how he was going to make an example out of Johnson. As I stood there hearing all this, I knew there was absolutely nothing I could do, and I knew I could not go back and tell Johnson that I truly knew what was going on. When Johnson came to me during the process and told me he thought he was going to get no divisional support and get screwed by the system, all I could do was stand there and listen. I knew his fate, and I knew he was right

As his career was coming to a close, Johnson came to my house to talk to Diane and I. He had a copy of his evaluations with him. He started reading it to me, and he kept saying, man, I can't believe they're doing me like this, I can't believe they wrote these things about me. All I can do is sit there and listen because I was the one who wrote all that stuff. That was probably the toughest time in my Navy career on dealing with some tough leadership issues, but again, as Mr. Rin had stated, this is what leadership is all about.

I saw now what the system was all about: The movers and shakers. To be invited into that inner circle, I knew I had risen to the right level. When I first got my head nod of acceptance to be a part of this group of movers and shakers, when you recognize the key people who are making things happen around you or whose words get the real attention, then take note because these are the individuals you may want to affiliate with during your quest to achieve success in your surrounding area. In my particular situation, there were a couple of E9s and E8s that had the ear of the Commanding Officer. I went home so excited.

I told Diane about what was going on in the system. Again, Rule #15: *In marriage, effective communication is paramount.* I said to her, "I get to play this game with the big boys." The caveat was, "Either you win in the game, or you lose." What losing meant was the end of a Navy career. I then asked her, can you handle me playing this game?"

"I trust you," she said, "And I know you know what you're doing."

I had her support, and I knew I could move forward as a team member through the next level of the Navy and leadership. Since discovering how the system works it's been a very joyous thing for me because I get to look back and see all the times I recognized what the system was and how to play in the system. You'll know when you've been accepted. I remember getting one of my first head nods clearly after I had figured out the system and it was a very exhilarating feeling to know that I made it over the first hurdle. I'm now in the boys club. But you have to still remember there are rules in the club and you can never break the rules because you'll be thrown out of the club just as quick as you were let into it.

In the Inner Circle, I was told about situations and people on the base, but I was sworn to secrecy. I was engaging Rule of the System #9: *Stay close to your circle, which should be extremely small.* Shortly after being accepted into the club, I was nominated and selected as a sailor of the quarter. The first time I was nominated for sailor of the quarter, during the selection process I did not get the final selection. This process is comprised of Chief Petty Officers E7 through E9 selecting the up-and-coming hotshot E6. I knew I was better than my contender (I didn't understand the game at that time), but I was told don't worry about it. The guy they selected needed to make rank before me because he had the time and needed to get promoted. I was so young in my career and had time. I didn't make a fuss about it despite my disappointment. I started to learn what this game was all about.

The next quarter, I was nominated and selected again, this time during the selection board process, the questions were easy softballs and the process was very quick. Across the street from the Commanding Officer's building was a club called the Top Four Club. After the interview, I was told congratulations; you are our newest selection. I went the fifty yards to the Top Four Club, and in the club was a huge banner congratulating me for my selection. I believe in miracles, but this was ridiculous. The magic of comprising a banner this quick was impossible. There's absolutely no way they could have designed and created a banner as elaborate as this in the time it took for me to leave the Commanding Officer's building and walk fifty yards to the club.

My selection as the Sailor of the Quarter was predestined. I had impressed all the right people who allowed me into the inner circle, and they saw me as an up-and-coming superstar. They had already chosen me. Now I know how the system works.

I continued my journey there in the Philippines, working hard to have an exceptional military career, which included not getting caught up into what was out in town. I witnessed first-hand and was part of an officer getting sold up the river for one offense, and I intended to play it smart so nothing would get in the way of my trajectory.

14 ~ USS KINKAID DD 965: OPERATING IN THE SYSTEM

After surviving the ousting of president Marcos shortly after arriving in the Philippines, all the crazy lessons about leadership in the shop, and the increased unrest in the Philippines, I was ready to leave after serving a three-year assignment. There were attacks on American soldiers, sailors, and airmen approximately one year after President Marcos was exiled off the island. It was time to go. We came on a hot December day, and three years later we left on a hot December day. Our destination was San Diego, California. I had lived in California before I met Diane. Now I would return a different person; married with a child. My assignment was on the USS Kinkaid DD 965, a destroyer. The Spruance class destroyer's primary mission was submarine hunting. Due to my background, I typically wasn't assigned to ships. The equipment I worked on was too sensitive for ships, so most of my time was spent in shore stations. I had no experience of what it was like to serve on a small boy (destroyer). The advice I had received from my leadership in the Philippines and my detailer was that if I wanted to be promoted, I had to serve some time on a ship.

Diane and I originally wanted to be stationed back on the East Coast, where all our family resided from Connecticut down to Georgia, but my detailer had a different idea. I liked San Diego before, so how bad could it be? Our first night back in San Diego, I wanted to show Diane the area I thought was the coolest place to live: National City. This neighborhood was within walking distance of the base. Therefore, I had not seen all of San Diego. I took Diane and child in the car, and we were going out to see the city, and as we drove down Highland Avenue, on just about every corner, the police had someone held up or pulled over, or had a gun drawn on them. I felt as if we were in a war zone. I quickly understood that National City or Chula Vista was fine once upon a time for a young single sailor, but were not suitable for my family.

It was a cool December evening in 1988 when we arrived in San Diego on a Friday evening, and I went to check-in on board the ship. Unbeknownst to me as I was walking across the gangway, they were lifting it to set out to sea for a weekend detail. Back then, I had no way of contacting Diane to let her know what was going on, so here I was heading to sea for the weekend and no communications with the family. Welcome to the USS Kinkaid! On Monday evening, when we returned, I quickly got off the ship and raced to let my Diane know what happened. Cell phones were not that popular back then, which made communicating a little different than now.

The next day I go back on board the Kinkaid to start my career officially on this illustrious ship. The crew was lazy and unconcerned about the ship. The Commanding Officer was clueless. The division I was assigned to had some of the worst torpedoman's mates and sonar technicians in the Navy. Every day of the week before the start of the day, we had quarters, which is when everyone gets together in formal ranks and talks about the events of the day (called the plan of the day.) Quarters are held at 8 a.m., and reveille happens at 6:30 am every day. I'm the new guy who is a military-strict rules follower, but I learned half the men in my department would show up late for quarters, or not at all.

Some would be sleeping in late, some would get to the ship on time and wouldn't be dressed properly. It was a team like the Bad News Bears on a ship. I was the senior E6 guy and had experience from the Philippines being a Leading Petty Officer, so I was chosen once again to be the Leading Petty Officer of this group. I began to learn what the system teaches about understanding your surroundings, your responsibilities, and your authority. When the system grants you access, you need to be very aware of what it means. One of the fallacies people fall prey to is that they get into the system and all of a sudden they think they are the top dog. This thinking will bring them down quicker than you can shake a stick. So you have to be grateful, humble, and move cautiously within your boundaries and your authority. You mustn't get too big for your britches. There are some who do that once they get accepted into the system. First, they try to expose the system, and then try to use the system to their advantage. These are the people who don't fare well in the system. Every now and then someone slips through the cracks.

In the system, you have to produce to get recognized, but once you're recognized, you will rise to the top very quickly. Upon my arrival on board the USS Kinkaid, once I was officially designated as the LPO, I quickly showed leadership to receive recognition. I showed commitment to the ship right away. I was up every morning at 6:30 and down in the birthing areas for when it was time for the crew to get up. I would wake them and ensure they were dressed. I would ensure they were at Quarters on time. My boss, who was a Senior Chief, was blown away. He had never seen someone at my level take charge of the situation and make it happen. My spaces were extremely clean and my uniform and my team were always squared away.

The system was working in my favor because I was the ship's Golden Boy. I arrived on board a U.S. Navy warship with aviation wings, which was definitely different than anyone had seen, and then shortly thereafter I received my Enlisted Surface Warfare Specialty (ESWS) pin. Because I had an aviation warfare pin and a surface warfare pin, I was a unique individual at this time. I had all the mojo working in my favor. Whenever the Commanding Officer had guests on board the ship, he would call me up to show me off as if I was some sort of piece of equipment, and then he would show how clean my spaces were. I could do no wrong. One of the critical lessons I learned along the way was when you go to a new command, you do everything by the books and do everything right. You do everything that's asked of you. If you do that within the first three months of your arrival, you will set a precedent that will last throughout your entire tour. Your character now has been defined and everyone thinks highly of you. They don't see the potential wrong that could be in you.

When I initially started, I got a little push back, but the military teaches you leadership. It teaches you the carrot and the stick. So I use a lot of stick and a little carrot. In layman's terms, I was more direct with my orders to them. I strictly held the men accountable with consequences, but when they started conforming, I praised them in public (the carrot). This worked for the few folks who resisted. The stick helped them come online pretty quick because they knew the results would not be to their advantage and that their careers could were on the line. I wasn't giving anyone extra chances. I was pretty rigid initially to get them all on the right track. This phase lasted about two months or so. Then I didn't have to go and wake them up because they knew the consequences.

My Senior Chief bragged about me all the time, and the Captain thought I was the best sailor ever. Here I was again, looking at one of the most crucial Rules of the System in my life trajectory again, Rule #1: *Seek, Identify, and appreciate your mentors. They have been put in your life to push you to greatness.* All the officers recognized me. Whenever we had visitors come on board the ship, they would always come to my spaces because they were the cleanest on board the ship. I was responsible for the torpedo magazines. Keep in mind I have no shipboard experience; all I could fall back on were my Philippines lessons learned about running a tight workshop.

The time came to deploy for a six-month Western Pacific Cruise; what we call West Pac. On West Pac, you typically had a couple of ports en route, but your primary mission was in the Persian Gulf. During this time, the country was dealing with escorting merchant ships through the Straits of Hormuz. We had the threat of Iran with their silkworm missiles. They launched them at military and merchant ships. We had to train and prepare for what we would be up against while making this voyage.

The Commanding Officer had some really weird ideas while we were at sea. He would have us go to General quarters and fire every weapon on board the ship at the same time. We were shooting at absolutely nothing. Instead of using this time wisely and doing real target practice, we were wasting ammunition so he get the thrill of hearing all the guns shoot at the same time. As a weapons person, this was a pain in the butt because when you shot the weapons, then they had to be cleaned. The Commanding Officer also had little experience in being a Commanding Officer, and it showed. He would walk around the ship and ask young sailors questions he should have known the answers to. I felt a great sense of unease when I understood this was the situation I was working under on board the Kinkaid.

As the Commanding Officer, he should know everything about the ship. He is the be-all-end-all, and if he doesn't know the ship, then there's no one else to turn to. How is the rest of the crew supposed to be guided if he's not the one? He lost so much respect from the crew that whenever he was on the microphone making announcements, people would listen to his announcement and count the number of times he said "uh." His messages were never heard, which means the information was not being disseminated across the ship. One time he did have a message that was very heartfelt and made sense. He was a history major, maybe even a military history major. We were sailing through the Straits of the Philippines on the Fourth of July. The skies were blue, and the clouds were white, and the sun was a fiery red. We had music playing in the background, Lee Greenwood's song "Proud To Be An American," and the Commanding Officer read a history of Independence Day and other war or military events that happened many years ago on the Fourth of July. With his description of this day in history, you felt proud to serve on a U.S. warship heading into harm's way.

Travel time is a month from San Diego to the Persian Gulf. We were at sea for quite some time. We entered into the Straits of Hormuz going into the Persian Gulf with the ship at its highest readiness state called General quarters or GQ. When at GQ, the ship is ready to fight. To go through the Straits of Hormuz, the country of Oman challenged our intentions. As a U.S. Navy warship, we had to ensure that our intentions were peaceful. A few ships ahead of us entered the straits carrying sheep and dumped all the dead sheep into the sea. A thousand dead sheep were floating on the water. The sight was eerie, and a sign of bad luck. Even after relieving from General quarters, the crew was still in an uneasy state.

In the Persian Gulf, we were assigned Patrol sections. The Gulf was divided into three patrol sections: The north, middle, and southern sectors. Our sector was the southern Persian Gulf. Other U.S. Warships were in the region, and our purpose there was to keep an eye on Iran and Iraq primarily, but also to escort ships through the Straits of Hormuz. We monitored their radio traffic and watched out for different shipping activities. Our biggest concern for contention on the seas were pirates. In this role, we ended up escorting over thirty-five ships through the Straits. Our longest General Quarters (GQ) was about twenty-two hours, which is extremely taxing on a crew.

We had some situations where we had some near collisions because the officers on board the ship did not respect the Commanding Officer. They built their little fiefdoms and never reported these incidents to him. This was also allowed within the enlisted ranks. The Captain himself had his little favorites who could do no wrong. The Commanding Officer had standing orders for all the bridge watch standers, but they were not followed properly. He did not hold his officers accountable. The fact that he did not know what was going on with his crew was scary. Because of this attitude, this made things questionable. The Commanding Officer did not have complete control of the crew and what was happening on board the ship. He created an environment that allowed other officers and senior enlisted personnel to build little groups that were not in line with his orders. Some call these cliques, and because of this, having confidence in his leadership was challenging, especially while serving in a dangerous place like in the Persian Gulf. It was very taxing on your mental status.

It is theoretically impossible for a Navy ship to have a collision at sea. The only way for it to happen is every watch station, every rule, *everything* needs to be violated at the same time. If the redundancies are not in place and followed, a calamity of errors is set up to lead to a major destructive event. Poor leadership was in place on this ship, and no one was being held accountable for their actions.

Later down the road when his system failed, it cost him his career. His failure catapulted my career. I still had to stay below the radar and maintain strong integrity and character. The lesson here is even when accepted into the system, if the system around you breaks down, you still have to be solid to maintain your future. If not, you could easily get caught up into the crumbling of the system around you.

15 ~ Collision at Sea: The Transition of Realities

As our time in the Gulf came to an end, the crew was exhausted. There were several close calls with the opposition in the Gulf, and pirates as well, among other things. During this particular cruise, we escorted tankers through the straits of Hormuz more than thirty-five times, which meant being at General Quarters, which is a state of full combat-readiness, sometimes for more than twenty hours at a time. After three months of combat-readiness, we were truly ready to go home, and the Commanding Officer allowed the ship to go into a very relaxed status. The men walked around in t-shirts, not in proper uniforms. As we later learned, this was a very dangerous decision. We were a warship; the ship's defensive guard should never come down to a level such as this as we headed home.

On a Westpac or Mediterranean cruise, ships typically sail with either a battle group or just one other ship, which is called MEF Steaming. We were MEF steaming with one other ship, the USS Rentz. The military believes there is safety in numbers. Both ships have an individual schedule they must keep and are responsible for their ship's movement and mission. On the journey home, we stopped at ports along the way, and the crew was excited about getting some R&R in Thailand. Because of the high-stress level in the Gulf, they truly let their hair down. When it was time to leave Thailand, we did not find our Master Chief of Command (CMC). Our MEF partner, the USS Rentz left on time to stay on schedule; we stayed behind to try and find the CMC. Four hours later, we discovered the CMC on the beach, drunk. Instead of the Commanding Officer at this point relieving him on the spot, he again swept it under the rug.

Missing ship's movement is a significant issue, and is a crime under the Uniform Code of Military Justice (UCMJ), and the Master Chief should have been relieved of command immediately.

Four hours behind schedule, we were sailing without our MEF Steaming partner and going through the Straits of Malacca, one of the most dangerous transits in the world, at a much faster rate than we had planned. Because we accelerated our travel, we got there earlier, and the Navigator never made the connection. Now we are there an hour early with the most inexperienced crew at the helm, myself included as the Junior Officer of the Deck. The watch team was thinking it was very busy around here. What is going on? And to add to it we are on the other side of the "road." I was the second-in-command of the bridge team. My role was to give steering orders to the helmsman and recommendations to the Officer of the Deck. The Officer of the Deck's position was to look at the overall situational awareness with the movement of the ship and provide guidance and direction to the bridge team through me. You also have the Combat Information Center (CIC) Watch Officer who runs the combat information center. Between the three of us, we had a total of three months' experience, one for each of us. Due to the delay caused by the drunken Command Master Chief, we were in a less than normal watch routine and in a situation that higher authority should have been manning.

I had been watching ships that were potentially dangerous to us, and I reported it to the Officer of the Deck. He in turn would report those events to the Commanding Officer, but because the behavior on the ship was keeping secrets from him, this information never reached him. The Commanding Officer was in his bunkroom asleep, oblivious to what was going on, as well as was the Navigator, when we arrived into the straits. The watch crew in CIC was split in half against the CIC Watch Officer's direction. Half were in their racks sleeping, and the other half were standing watch with white lights on. White lights on at night on a Navy ship affects your ability to have night vision; at night, the only approved lighting is red lighting. The CIC watch team was breaking all the rules. Technically, because just left a mission zone, we should have still been in a state of readiness. We should have been properly manned at our watch stations, but we were not. The office of the deck and the CIC Watch Officer became involved and distracted, looking for a buoy to orient our direction, not realizing the ship was on the wrong side of the traffic scheme. It was unbelievable that they did not want to hear anything concerning the ship's movement. I was the only one looking at ship traffic, and no one was validating what I was witnessing.

"Ship A has a close point approach of 300 yards and 20 knots," I told the Officer of the Deck, and that two other ships were a major concern to us. They would be passing us inside the comfort zone and violating the standing orders from the Commanding Officer. When I reported this to them, they (the OOD and the CIC Watch Officer) should have awakened the Captain and let him know what was going on.

He was not interested in anything I was saying, and he told me to shut up.

"You have no idea what you are talking about. Just drive the ship!" he said.

For fifty-five minutes, I drove. Finally, I screamed at him, "This ship is going to hit us!"

He felt we were in an overtaking situation, but we were in a crossing situation. By the time he realized I was right in my alarm, it was too late.

A Panamanian register tanker hit us on the right side of the ship, right in the side of my pristine torpedo magazine. The Navigator was killed instantly, and four of my best friends were sucked out into the Straits of Malacca. The fuel tanks were ruptured poured fuel into the water. You had two ships side by side and your four men in the water between the two ships. Our ship was on fire, men were hurt, and the Officer of the Deck lost personal control. He was literally jumping up and down in fear. He completely freaked out, continuously saying, "Oh my God, how many men have I killed?" He became utterly useless.

We fought the fire for at least several hours. We were able to recover the men out of the ocean without any major injuries. One of the men had two broken legs, and the others had ingested some of the fuel. We were able to assess the damage of the ship once the fires were out. The ship was almost broken in half. Needless to say, because I had to enter the magazine where I knew there were live torpedoes, I thought my time had come to die at sea.

In a way, this collision had already happened the day we left San Diego. What I mean by this is that a series of events happened throughout the cruise, most of which went unchallenged, or people were not held accountable. There was a calamity of things that built-up to the final act, which was the collision. It took just four months for the laziness and ineptitude of the senior officers to build up and come to a head and have everything that could go wrong happen at the same time. Luckily, our damage-control team and ship's crew did a great job getting the water pumped and doing some damage control in time before we began to sink.

Once we were able to get everything under control, we were able to limp the ship along to Singapore for repairs. The investigations commenced immediately with an Admiral arriving on board the ship the second day after the collision with his team. The crew was all shaken up, anxious, tired, and wanted to go home, but that wasn't going to happen any time soon. This experience tormented me. I lost everything I owned; the ship hit right where my bunk was located. I became the primary witness against the caption, OOD, and the CIC Watch Officer. I lost faith in the Navy. I lost faith in the leadership. I lost faith in the rules I had created. I was ready to get out.

The Singapore shipyard installed what is called a finger patch. A finger patch is basically putting a steel plate over the gaping hole that was on the side of the ship. This temp repair allowed the ship to sail from Singapore to the Philippines. The entire bridge team had to see a psychiatrist while in Singapore. This visit to the shrink was very important. This event was very traumatic. When it was my turn to meet with the mental health doctor, he asked my thoughts, and I asked him to recommend to the Commanding Officer that I be discharged from the Navy immediately. He did not honor my request, and instead, he told the Commanding Officer that I should get back on the bridge as soon as possible.

At this time of my life, the last thing I needed to hear was to get back on the horse that threw you. I was over the Navy. Shortly after the Collision, the Commanding Officer was relieved of command. The only officer whose career was not individually affected through this ordeal was the Executive Officer and me. All the other officers who were involved had their careers come to an abrupt end. Even some enlisted personnel careers came to an end. One particular sailor was a loaner from another ship, but because he was a part of the navigation department, the Navy had to hold someone accountable since the Navigator was dead. It became very apparent how disposable we all were. We were pawns for the Navy, and that made me realize how insignificant we were in the big scheme of things. We were just numbers on a paper written in pencil.

After having the tragic event of the collision, it was time to clean up and blame. The Navigator was killed in the incident, so he was clearly not available to receive any punishment for the lack of his duty. The next person in line who had nothing to do with his decision had to take the fall because someone had to be blamed. The system is unforgiving and did not care that this young man had nothing to do with the events that happened; the Navy had to blame someone and hold someone accountable. He was the unfortunate individual targeted by the Navy. The dead guy received kind words, but others around him had their careers destroyed. For my entire career up to this point, I had been proud to be part of the Navy. Now I felt like it was a big career mistake.

After all the major repairs, we ended up returning to San Diego ten months after our original departure. The families were worried, and the crew was worn out. My family personally had to deal with some pretty harsh circumstances. I found out upon my return that when the news media reported that a U.S. Navy ship was involved in a collision at sea and someone died, they did everything they could to get a story. When it was discovered I was the Conning Officer (ship driver) and my family was local in San Diego, the media camped out in front of my house, trying to get a story from my wife. She knew she had to be silent about the events; anything she would say would go on record. My family was traumatized. They went through a lot, but we overcame the ordeal.

Even though I wanted to leave the Navy, I had somehow remained positive and knew I was on the right side of the system. After this died down, the system was now working for me in my favor. I had such a great reputation because I had established myself immediately after the event. An individual had me sit down and write everything that happened and helped me publish an article. Now it would have looked bad for the Navy to crucify the individual who tried to do the right thing. When the Admiral came on board and heard the story of what I had done, he told me not to worry about a thing. There were others in who vouched for me to say I knew what I was doing. I had credibility.

When the investigations were completed, I was told I was the only individual who had clear situational awareness of what was happening while the ship was going through the straits and how it was a shame no one listened to me and was told to shut up during the ordeal. We lost a very good man that day and a great Navy Officer all the crew admired. Four of my friends today are still affected by what happened on November 12, 1989, at 5:18 a.m. That day was also my wife's birthday. What a birthday present to give to the one you love.

When a ship goes through an ordeal, in most cases, the Commanding Officer is brought up on criminal charges or neglect. In either case, they have to go through a general court-martial. This process is a military court hearing. I was used in the system to turn against my Commanding Officer. He was charged with criminal negligence and the system used me to verify the fact he didn't do what he was supposed to do according to the rules and regulations. Me testifying wasn't a right or wrong decision. I was illustrating the facts according to the rules and regulation from the position I was in. However, I was a live body testifying against the current situation, so much so that I was even told along the way i did not have anything to worry about—I just had to go along with the process and I would be okay. Because of this ordeal, I received my commission as a naval officer shortly after the collision. Rule of the System #6 was critical here for my career to continue forward: *Own your mistakes but don't take the fall for others.*

After returning to the ship and going through all of the court martial trials, we were back to business as usual. It was difficult to serve on that ship for the next year with the residual trauma I endured, but I did. I learned after this ordeal that you have to face your fears to keep ascending to the next level in life. When you stare down that which scares you the most, you are no longer blocked from the good life and can learn to be the person you've always dreamed about in your mind: Your ideal self. Finding your courage is a life-changing decision. Fear will always be around to tell you what you can't do—it's up to you to face your fears, and tell yourself you can do it. No matter what, it's always scary to go to a place that's unknown, especially as you climb up the leadership ladder. Your main fear is whether or not you're capable of doing the job. Others around you who selected you know you are capable; you just have to believe in yourself.

Some people would have stopped after this collision and ended their careers, and that would have been their final peak. I had to regain my disposition and composure on that ship and re-establish my honor and integrity. I had to re-boot my belief system with all I had seen and experienced in my life. I had to remind myself that what happened had little to do with me adhering to my rules. I couldn't control the ineptitude of others. Some sailors faulted me, and some sailors supported me. Some said I could have done more to save the ship, and some knew I did all I could do.

I left the Kinkaid in February of 1991 and was assigned to the Fleet Training Group in San Diego, just about twelve miles from where the Kinkaid was berthed. My job at this new command was to go out and inspect ships and train the officers in their ability to manage damage control procedures as if they were in a real battle or a collision—the very experience I just lived through. We would be assigned a schedule of several ships to go out and train. We would know well in advance how many ships, how many days it would take and what type of training we have to do. If you were not training a ship, you were at home.

This new command was exactly what I needed after a tour on board the Kinkaid. Because my tour there was limited, I found out two weeks after my arrival I had been selected to get my officer commission. From that point forward, I was waiting to be commissioned, which is roughly a three-year process. I could have just sat back and marked time, but I was engaging. I took on more responsibilities. I trained hard and held the ships we inspected accountable for their understanding of damage control. I took the lead role in some or most of the training missions. I continued to work hard, get involved in the political system there at that command, and earned respect and admiration as the go-to guy. When you go into a new environment, you have to quickly establish yourself and earn some credibility. The old adage that a first impression is a lasting impression is so true. As you're moving up the ladder, you have to be conscientious of that first impression.

16 ~ FLEET TRAINING GROUP: BEAT OUT NUMBER ONE

In anticipation of being commissioned, I had to close out my enlisted career items, prepare to move my family overseas, and temporarily locate them during my time in officer's commissioning school. There was quite a bit going on in my life at this time. One of the first things to consider was the planning of the upcoming transfer to Cuba. We needed to find a renter for my home and buy a different car we could drive across the country and take overseas. Not to be seen as an individual just hanging out at the new command, I had to be strategic in my actions. I had to gain creditability at the new command even if it was only for a short while. I also needed to manage the time off I had in this new environment. What I would gain from this short period of time being in this environment I didn't think would bode well for me, but no matter where you're at and no matter how long or how little you're there, you always have to do your best. It turned out the Commodore who I worked for at this location was an individual I would see later down my path. He knew me, so he gave me more respect than he gave the Commanding Officer of the ship I went to after my tour at Fleet Training Group (FTG) San Diego.

As I had understood, in this new system with gaining respect and creditability, my first strategic move was to find out who was the number one guy at my level I could beat out for that spot. Now this is not something you say out loud to anyone. You internalize this goal in the system, and you factor it into your strategy as you are now beginning to navigate through the new jungle. At this point, I am trying to apply all fifteen Rules of the System to my daily operations. You then map out your future, beginning with the end in mind and have a prepared contingency plan if your original plan fails.

Not that It mattered. After all, my fate was already determined there, but I still had to play the game. The first appropriate step was to meet the command master chief. During my in-brief to the new command, I asked the Master Chief of Command who was the number one guy and what would I need to do to become the number one guy. I learned early in my quest to be the best you can be, and I was not afraid of bold statements as a brand-new individual who's at the command only to get Commissioned. I started a philosophical discussion about what was going on in the command and what I needed to do for recognition. Instead, what I received from this guy was the importance of the command and the base parking situation. He talked to me for two hours straight about where to park my car, how to park, what to do when you park and what not to do, what time to park, and so on. I sat there listening to him dumbfounded. I was trying to become the number one sailor at this command, and all I got for feedback from this superior Chief Petty Officer was where to park around the building.

When the discussion was over, I walked away scratching my head, asking myself what in the heck just happened. I went back to my group of colleagues, and I asked what they thought about this Command Master Chief. They told me how useless he was, which was rather sad, considering I was all fired up just coming from the Kinkaid and what I had been through while on board. I had little to no tolerance for incompetent people after seeing men die, and now I was coming to a command that had the same type of CMC. I would figure out how to get the position of number one without the Master Chief's advice. I began to volunteer for the hard jobs that were not assigned to me. I asked for training above and beyond and made myself visible with the Commodore as needed. Part of my strategy was to get to know the Commodore and for the Commodore to get to know who I was. His recognition meant more to me than anyone else at the command because he was at the very top of the food chain. So part of my lessons learned is it's good to know who's who in the zoo, but it's even more important to know the zookeeper.

The good news was that I was well-liked immediately by my team. Simply because I did not pose a threat to any of them, I only enhanced the things they were doing. The guys were a cast of characters, but at the time, we were all E7 through E9. To sit around with this group of men was interesting all in itself. Within our team, we had guys who were hotshots and wanted to do more in their career, and on the other hand we had guys who were coasting along waiting for retirement.

During my time at the new command, I had the opportunity, I thought, to take on a second job telemarketing. I lasted only one week in that environment. All day long, I was cold calling people from a list trying to get them to subscribe to some magazine. It was a comedy, but in this job, some people were truly very good at sales. We had a status board in the area where we all worked, and whoever became the number one salesman or woman would get some crazy perk. I'm not sure exactly what it was, but it didn't excite me. At the end of my first week on this job, I turned in my resignation and decided that as an active-duty Navy person, having a second job was not in my best interest.

Remodeling my condo was a better idea. I had no idea what I was doing, but I had a lot of time to figure it out. Although my wife was pregnant with our second daughter, she still worked all day, and my first daughter was in EK (Early Kindergarten), so I had a tremendous amount of time on my hands. Letting my mind wander and my imagination take control, the remodeling began. Once I purchased all the right tools and had a really good understanding of what it was that I was doing, the plan started coming together and worked out well. I learned later that my neighbor across the street was a general contractor. He knew all about what I was trying to do. I enlisted his help. He was quite an interesting guy because he loved to drink beer, so for me the cost of his time was keeping cold beer around.

During this time of my life, it was very interesting. I had the remodeling going on at my home, the desire to be number one at my command, and more time on my hands than I knew what to do with while stationed there at FTG. My neighbor's name was Mike, and Mike's daughter was the same age as my oldest daughter, the two of them played together from time to time, and I got to know the family pretty well. Mike gave me some great pointers. I ripped out all the carpet in the house, ripped out all the paneling, and started making some adjustments. I would do the work and then I have Mike come back and inspect it to make sure I did it correctly. Everything was going well. My wife found a job to start a new career, my oldest daughter had friends in school, and this job I had gave me more time off than I could ever imagine. Life was good.

Up until now I had been learning about the system and how the system could make or break you—how the system can be good or bad and when to observe and not participate in many facets of it. Part of your observation when you're involved in a new system is to sit in the bleachers and watch the show. You don't always have to participate, especially if you have to put something in the game. You do have the right to reserve judgement and to not get involved and just drive alongside, learn, and watch what's happening in the system that surrounds you.

Now when you're in the system, you should know better as to what's in front of you, what's beside you, and what's around you so you remember how the system is unforgivable. For just when life is cruising along, and all the parts fit perfectly in place, everything is aligned, a game-changing life lesson is lurking. I had seen enough of career and life ups and downs to justify being nervous. This time, I wasn't watching anyone not do their job like on the Kinkaid before the disaster. I just knew a disaster was waiting to happen. I also learned at this time that I had a certain level of premonitions—not that I think that I'm psychic or anything like that—just one of those things where you know something is going on around you, whether it's clear or not. You need to be aware. The lesson here is to pay attention to that little voice in your head. This is the same voice we all laugh about and ignore, and sometimes we call this our sixth sense.

I had heard this little voice before in the past, but I ignored it in some cases, and every time I ignored it something bad would happen. For example, my first wife, there were a lot of red flags and a lot of little voices I ignored. My tour in Charleston with the drug situation I was involved in had a lot of little voices I ignored, but I was lucky because I didn't do anything horrible or get caught, which could have changed my life forever. But now, having been through the events on the Kinkaid, I learned to respect those little voices. Whenever that little voice would whisper something in my head, I at least recognized there was a little voice. I didn't always act on it but at least I was aware. I had no idea what that disaster was around the corner that I did not want to focus on now. I just put it in the back of my mind. I just knew there was something out there lurking and I would find out about it soon enough.

The first event was Mike just up and died. Thursday night he went home and had dinner with his wife, Lynn. She said when she went to bed at about 1:00 a.m. Mike started coughing violently. Then he sat up in bed and just toppled over, dead. Later we learned Mike had a massive heart attack at the age of thirty-five. His daughter, Alicia, showed no emotions; she was in shock, I believe. She was just a young eight or nine-year-old girl who just lost her dad. There was no way for her to process what had just happened to her father. I was mortified, stunned, and I had no idea what to think. Of course, we went over and consoled Lynn as best we could. Thirty-five years old and to drop dead of a massive heart attack—it started putting some perspective on my life. I thought about the Kinkaid. I thought about bike tours in Charleston. I thought about how precious life truly is. But I was still pretty relentless about pursuing my career. I knew I had commissioning coming and I knew I still had to do a good job for United States Navy.

After the Mike situation, I was taking on all the hard jobs, asking for extra assignments, and took the personal initiative to accomplish becoming certified as a Master Training Specialist. I did not need this designation, but what else could I do while waiting for my command? Besides, I thought it would be fun being number one, even if it would be very short-lived. A few months passed and things were going well, and again that little voice in the back of my head was saying I'm still not satisfied, even with the training we were doing on new techniques to help a ship understand what would happen if they were to get hit by a missile. I was pretty geared up about this.

Then my grandmother passed away.

My grandmother was always very important in my life, and I am her namesake. She lived in Georgia on our farm. She was a very smart businesswoman for her time who had no formal education yet managed to capitalize on opportunities when they presented themselves. The farm in Georgia has been in the family since the early 1800s, and she ensured she did all the right things to pass it down to my siblings and me. I always loved going to visit and sit and listen to her wise counsel, her reminiscences of life when she was a little girl. She was born in 1895 before there were any airplanes, trains, automobiles, or even electric lights. I loved talking to her about living in those times. It seemed like things were much simpler then but also just as complicated as now. It was a different kind of complexity or simplicity.

This news paralyzed me. The drive home was about thirty minutes, and it was the longest thirty-minute drive of my life. What was daunting about the drive was I could not hold back the tears, I was crying all the way home. My Grandmother was my world. I didn't know what to do. I didn't know what to say. I didn't know what to think. The little voice in the back of my head had let me know to prepare for this news. This was the first time in my life someone very close to me died. Back in July 1970, when my aunt passed away, it wasn't devastating because I didn't know her. The only time I ever saw my aunt was in her casket, but my grandmother was a different story. We were able to get things together and quickly get a flight out of San Diego. We were sitting in Georgia the next day after receiving the news. My family dynamics are interesting, probably like most American families—dysfunctional. My mother was beside herself because she was the last living child. Both my aunt and uncle were shot and killed in Jacksonville, Florida. My uncle had passed away before I was born. I never knew him. I never knew my grandfather either, but my grandmother cherished the idea I was following my grandfather's footsteps in the Masonic order.

When I received my 32nd degree in Masonry, my grandmother gave me a pillowcase she had sewn for my grandfather years ago when he was coming up through the ranks. This pillowcase was the journey he took, and it was the same journey I had taken. The amazing thing about this was that I had no idea that my grandmother knew I was doing what he did, and it was very coincidental, I thought. When I completed all of the degrees, she gave that pillowcase to me. Now I have that pillowcase encased in glass in a floating frame hanging on my wall in my home today. My grandmother was very intuitive. She knew all the things I was doing when I thought no one knew. My grandmother taught me about character and the importance of never lying, cheating, or stealing. She drilled that into my head. I never spent extended time with a liar, a thief, or a rogue. Surely in my Navy career, I had encountered some of those types of people. But because of her instilled wisdom I always quickly moved to get my distance from them. Her lessons in morality have served me well.

Instead of trying to figure out if you fit into one of these categories, you cut ties early and run and never regret the decision. She taught me about business in her little way. She was the lady in the neighborhood that sold candy for $0.25 to all the little kids. She also babysat a few kids. Today all the kids she babysat turned out to be successful individuals. My cousin, in particular, grew up to become an NFL football player for the San Francisco 49ers. He was very grateful and very thankful for his achievements. He did not have a big pompous head and was happy he had met his life goals. After talking to him and reflecting on my Navy career, I had perspective in terms of no matter how far you go, always remember where you come from.

I still keep my grandmother close to me. I know she lives within me, and she is that voice in my head of real deep strength I need to overcome obstacles and achieve success. After her service, it was time to head back to California to the fleet training group. Upon my return, I had a new perspective and a new outlook on life. I had to be as successful an officer as I could be. I had to be successful as a father, and I had to achieve greatness for my grandmother. She was one amazing woman, and I thank God for her. For her alone, I would carry on with the Rules of the System and be a success.

17 ~ Brush with Death

I was back riding ships again and training. I gave up on talking to the command master chief about the number one spot and just took it upon myself to work hard and achieve it all on my own. My best friend Larry, who also was getting a commission, went through officers indoctrination course with me down in Pensacola, Florida. The Officers indoctrination course was phenomenal. There were twenty-five type "A" personalities in one room together. What a very humbling experience. Our class average was 98.5%. It reminded me of the movie *Top Gun* when the commander asked who was the best officer and almost everyone in the class stood up. For the next eight weeks we were physically and mentally tested every week. Our families got to experience being in Pensacola during this amazing journey together.

In July 1992, it was commissioning day, and all the families flew out to see this great achievement. My mother and my mother-in-law pinned on my bars, and my wife assisted both of them while my children looked on. The major accomplishment in this story, which is usually unheard of, from a brand new E5 in the navy and seven years later being commissioned as an officer. This accomplishment is a very rare achievement in the Navy. The system works when you have the right rules, and by implementing them, all you have to do is be steadfast and believe. The system isn't fair or forgivable, but it's just. This system works. Why? It's been around since the beginning of time, and will continue to be around as long as people exist. Again, there are those who decide they don't want to comply, which is okay because not everyone is meant to keep growing, changing, and aspiring for more. You are reading this book to perfect what it is that you're seeking, so you have made a decision to have more in your life.

Larry and I still had our same 1992 Isuzu Rodeos, both in the color red. Larry's family flew down to Pensacola from Texas and got in safe. I had to drive from Pensacola, Florida to Atlanta, Georgia to pick up my wife and two kids and then drive back for the graduation from Officers Candidate School. On our return trip, I had been driving all day and was very tired. I decided to let my wife drive from Tallahassee into Pensacola. My oldest daughter asked if she could sit up front in the passenger seat beside my wife, and I said, of course, sure, and I sat behind my wife. As my wife got the vehicle up to speed (about 65 or 70 miles per hour), the back right tire blew. The car swerved back and forth and then started doing 360-degree circles on the highway and then tumbled on its side two or three times in a very violent accident. When the vehicle finally came to rest, the driver's side was lying on the highway, and the passenger side was up in the air. My youngest daughter was in her car seat suspended in the air and my oldest daughter was in the front seat locked in her seatbelt. The accident was amazing. One of the people who helped us out of the car kept saying we must have been a Christian family. She said she was behind us, and the way the car violently flipped then turned and twisted, there was no way anyone should have walked away alive. When the ambulance came, they were not in a big hurry because they thought they were coming to take away bodies, not injured people. They assumed it was nothing but fatalities in the vehicle.

The only injuries to my family were a few small cuts on my wife's left shoulder from the glass that was on the highway, and my oldest daughter had a small cut on her hand from someone pulling her out of the car. That evening, the state police took us to get a rental car and we got back on the road. We drove for about forty-five minutes and then decided to pull over and get a hotel room for the night.

I believe it dawned on my wife and I about the same time that we were in shock and finally began to understand what just happened. We also needed to call the families and let him know we had been in a terrible car accident, but everyone was okay. Graduation happened flawlessly, and the family and I went and got checked out medically. The doctors told us our children in the future will probably have problems going on violent rides and roller coasters at amusement parks. To date, that was far from the truth because they both enjoy roller coasters and crazy rides. This experience with the family brought us even closer together. We saw ourselves as a strong, cohesive unit. The entire experience brought about a whole new meaning to adventure and travel (a little humor). Our vehicle was totaled at the scene of the accident. We had to ride a train from Florida to Virginia.

With that said, we needed to catch a plane to Cuba from the naval base in Norfolk, Virginia. Before finishing what we call knife and fork school and right after learning about being selected, I received orders to naval base Gitmo Cuba as the base Ordnance Officer. Since we totaled our car, we still had to arrive at our new duty station on time. Our family calls ourselves The Griswolds, named after the movie *National Lampoon's Family Vacation*.

I understood in this episode in my life that I can have all the Rules down, but the essential piece is a strong team to be there while you understand, manage, and operate in the system. It is key you have a strong family bond and unity. As the head of the family, you have to do an awesome job in communicating everything that's happening. As you operate through the system, everyone has to be in sync. You can't afford distractions while you're trying to navigate through the system effectively. You can't have the wild child out doing drugs and getting in trouble, for example, while you try to navigate through the strategic waters of the system. You need your whole family on board.

18 ~ GUANTANAMO BAY: BRAND NEW NAVAL OFFICER

My next duty station as the base Ordnance Officer of Guantanamo Bay Cuba would be the true ultimate test of the system. All my talk about the Rules of the System, and the awareness and understanding of the system, would be ultimately tested in Cuba. What I know and understand is how "Life gives you the test first and then the lesson." This means we are tested every day of our life. There are simple choices we have to make, and then there are complex decisions we have to make. This quote reminds me we either reap the benefits of our decision or suffer the consequences. The example I taught my girls about this while they were growing up was when my oldest daughter was about 100 feet from an attacker who shot up Santana High School. A fourteen-year-old kid acting on a dare killed two kids and wounded thirteen others. His test was to act or not to act on a dare from peer pressure. He failed his test because he carried out the dare. His lesson: He was tried as an adult and sent to prison. He will not be eligible for patrol until he is sixty-four years old. That's a hefty price to pay for not understanding the system of life.

Guantanamo Bay was my first Duty station as a naval officer. The transition was swift. I was an enlisted Chief Petty Officer being responsible for only a division of sailors one day, and the next day a naval officer now responsible as a major Department Head. Because I was a major department head, all of my colleagues were more senior officers than I - Navy captains, commanders, and Lieutenant Commanders. I was a Chief Warrant Officer. All my years of experience as a Chief Petty Officer, I had no commissioned officer experience, but I had to perform at their level with no senior executive training and with no real senior executive experience. One thing the Navy teaches you is to survey the area you're responsible for as a naval officer. I already had this Rule of the System to survey the environment from my collective life experiences. In the Navy, when you get assigned to a new duty station you're required to walk in and within days become the resident expert. The only way you're going to do that is if in your first few days your immediate action is to survey the environment to see who's who. Again, this is very critical because you're seeking acceptance and buy-in from the powers that be. it is critical to pay attention to this because your first three months in a new environment are your defining months.

Then you operate in that space professionally. My first introduction to Cuba was doing my turnover with the prior Ordnance Officer. He drove me around, showing me the territory I would now be responsible for and the level of responsibility I would have, which increased a hundredfold. I was now responsible for over half of the base because half the base had bombs, bullets, mines, and other explosive weaponry on it (ordnance). We had active minefields around the base. We had nine different organizations or other commands we call tenant commands. I was responsible for their weapons and ammunition. There were the Marine guards that were leeward and windward that I was responsible for as well. As the former Ordnance Officer took me around, I saw some troubling things. Our first stop was at 10 a.m. to see my

Senior Chief of the division on the bay fishing, knowing I was his new boss checking in. This kind of lack of responsibility was my introduction to him. Seeing this on my first day did not go over very well with me.

My next visit was the ordinance garage, where my Quality Assurance Safety Officer resides; he was in charge of this area. He was sitting around with other officers like this was the local hang-out lounge. I went into his office only to find that the file cabinets were full of alcohol, one file cabinet had all your bourbons, another had all your gins, and so forth and so on. I looked in the refrigerator; I see beer and wine coolers and wine. This location is for vehicle maintenance and temporary park ordinance Leyden Vehicles. This situation I witnessed didn't sit well with me either. This group used this space as a little getaway, not realizing what they were jeopardizing with the potential of so many bombs being in the location. The criticality of the explosive ordnance garage was for planning work that was going on in this space and the movement of weapons. Drinking and carrying on in a very hazardous location was not a good idea. I also learned that the Executive Officer was using the garage as his personal painting booth. He and the Quality Safety Officer were painting cars and selling them for profit using military equipment to do this action. This is directly against the law. I could not believe they were running a car painting business out of the military ordnance garage.

My department was comprised of three divisions, a division of Jamaicans, a division of Gunner's mates, and a division of Aviation Ordnance men. I had a very large Department, and the most interesting aspect of my department was it was about 97% African American. This was the first experience I've ever had in my life working with so many of my own kind. I also was introduced to the base HR Director who I learned was having an affair with the QA Safety Officer. After my first day, I went home, shaking my head, wondering what I had got myself into. I knew this duty station was going to be a challenge, but I had no idea how much of a challenge it was going to be.

I went to what I know for dealing with all these dysfunctions: The Rules of the System. My first step was to have a meeting with the Commanding Officer and to give him a report on what I saw. I had to do that in order to establish a baseline of where I was and where I needed to go, and find out if he was going to support my efforts. I needed to know if I could trust his mentorship. I knew the Executive Officer who was the ringleader of the little group that hung out at the ordnance garage was not going to support me. I had to understand the support I would receive when navigating through the system. If I didn't have the Commanding Officer's endorsement, it would be very difficult for me to make it through the system against the Executive Officer. Having the Commanding Officer's support would bode well for me to achieve what I needed in my position. I identified and knew the players. If you have a player who is not on your side, you need to understand how to navigate around them to not let them torpedo your efforts.

To make matters worse, the Executive Officer was a redneck out of Alabama who, after thirty-five years of service in the Navy, was still a racist. My first-hand experience living in Georgia and seeing how people like him act informed me of this fact. I was astonished and blown away that he had been in the military as long as he had been and still carried these types of biases. I quickly recognized him for who he was, and I separated myself from him. I also learned that he and the QA Safety Officer were best friends. After I let the Commanding Officer also know what I saw with my turnover, seeing my Senior Chief on the fishing creek and seeing a bunch of alcohol at The ordnance garage, I let him know why I needed his support. He trusted me right off the bat. I took a gamble because he was new and I was new, and maybe he had heard some of the stories about Guantanamo Bay.

My first act of duty was to shut down the ordnance garage. When I did that, I made instant enemies of the crew that hung out there. That was fine by me because I knew I had a job to do and I knew if something happened all the responsibility would fall on my shoulders. I took on that responsibility. The Executive Officer was extremely upset with me because I didn't allow his friend to do what he wanted to do. At one point, he pulled me aside and threatened me and told me I had better leave this guy alone.

"Who does that guy work for?" I asked him.

"You, of course," he said.

"Well I won't be leaving him alone then," was my reply.

That really got him upset, and I knew from that point forth he was not a friend of mine. Luckily, through my smart communication using the system, the Commanding Officer liked me.

The next utilization of the system was to build a faction of friendships that were in the right mindset. In order for me to win in this particular system, I had almost become narcissistic in the sense of getting people to buy into what was going on with me. I needed to build my pool of allies. I made sure I was in good standing with the entire legal team and that we had a great relationship. I had to know their feelings toward the Executive Officer and what they thought him, if they knew he was unethical and would they help my cause when I was looking for support. Like playing chess, when working out a system element, every move you make has to be calculated and you must have an expected outcome as you move around the board.

The group of people I befriended was the Staff Judge Advocate and the entire legal team on the base. Rule of the System #10 applied immensely here: *Be discerning about whom you trust with your ambitions.* I also made friends in the personnel office, at the base of operations, and the Operations Officer. All these people were key individuals to know. I learned that the Admin Officer was a friend of the Executive Officer and also was a team member of the crew that hung out in the ordnance garage. This situation was getting very interesting and exciting because I knew I was walking into a figurative minefield and knew my career could potentially suffer from my actions, so I walked the line very carefully.

I got my entire department together and laid down the laws on what my expectations were. I made it very clear I did not like lazy people. If you wanted to get along with me, do your job to the best of your ability. I had a discussion with the Senior Chief about my disappointment and seeing him on the fishing creek as I was checking in. It was detrimental for that to be the example he was setting for the rest to follow; it was not the example I would expect from a senior enlisted. Another Chief Petty Officer who worked for me had some personality issues. Every morning when he came into work, he looked like someone had peed in his Wheaties. He would not say good morning to the troops; he would walk right in, go right into his office and sit down and not say anything. It was horrible. What I learned was that my predecessor was a drunk and just let everyone do what they wanted to do. I had a completely different leadership style. I was more of a hands-on get involved guy who understood processes, set examples, and generated momentum. They were not used to someone like me coming in. I understood I had to figure out how to make change in the department, and I had to do it delicately as best I knew how. I had to reach into my years of personnel experience, and reach back into the years of leadership to manage this as I went forward. Here is where learning and understanding the system paid off once I knew

I had the captain's confidence. I began to put my plan into action. I started holding people accountable, shut down the ordnance garage situation, and made my Senior Chief do his job.

As you move around the chess board of life and you build up your allied support, you have to know who will support you when times get tough. I had the Commanding Officer's confidence and trust, so I knew I could move a little more aggressively in the system. I still had to be very respectful to the Executive Officer. I could not treat him with disdain. I had to treat him with respect. Even though I knew I was winning in the system, I could not pound my chest and stand on the mountainside and shout. Rule of the System #4 demands humility. In the system, it's not important who publicly wins, or shall I say the public announcement as to who wins. The victor is the one who walks away with his head up, quietly knowing the aftermath wasn't a total shambles. The Executive Officer lost and I won.

Now that the tour began, I had to take an assessment of what we had on base as far as weapons and responsibilities. I had to assign people jobs and hold all them to high standards. We changed how we did business and when I thought we were doing well, I was happy. What happened was when I thought I had everything under control, there was an undertone of negativity happening right in front of my face and I didn't see it until it was almost too late. I trusted the Senior Chief Petty Officer named Bob within my department, so I thought I would try to educate him in the process early on. All along he had a different ulterior motive. If you find yourself in a similar situation with authority, you must be alert to your surroundings. Key red flags will sail around you that you have to acknowledge or it's on you if you fail. I almost missed these indicators of the players not on my team. Historically, as I look back, there have always been glaring red flags. You have to pay attention to them always or it's on you.

We had to move a large amount of ordnance (Bombs, missiles, and other explosives) on the base. While we're briefing the ship, I was assuring the captain of the ship we could have the ordnance on board in a relatively quick time. Without warning, my Senior Chief Bob pipes up.

"Sir, we're not even ready."

I was stunned and embarrassed by his undermining conduct as a junior individual in a discussion between the Captain of the Ship and myself. Be aware of who you trust: Rule of the System #12: *Don't let the haters distract you from your objectives.* In a case like this, if he disagreed with me, he should have waited until we were alone and then discussed his concerns in private, not publicly. My actions are always positive and aggressive with forward-thinking solutions. It was clear this Senior Chief and I did not see eye to eye.

A second incident occurred when I received a secret assignment to load ammunition in a non-ammo loading area. Instead of the Senior Chief understanding the mission orders, he was more concerned about not knowing the full request than following my orders. He went behind my back and turned me in to the Safety Officer for violating the explosive safety loading zones. Little did he know that the base Safety Officer and I were friends and she immediately called me up and told me what he was doing. This was strike six because what he did was very bad. Later it would cost him his career. I knew then I could not trust him or his judgment. Thinking he was smart and intelligent, which he was not, he tried to befriend the administrative officer who was a friend of the Executive Officer so he could go behind my back and do things, such as undermine my actions to lead the Department or get the crew to go against me. Unfortunately for him, it backfired, and I tried to tell him he put himself in a game he knew nothing about and he had no idea how the system worked.

The system is unforgiving and this particular case, the Senior Chief Petty Officer thought he could step into a level of the system when he did not know the rules. In order to try and take command of a situation, you need to have put in the work as an observer to know what system you're operating in and you truly have to know the players and the rules of what's happening around you. Here's a perfect example of an individual who perceived the system incorrectly and was used by more skillful players of the system. They took full advantage of his ignorance and at the end of the day his career ended. He was done and they moved on without a second thought about him.

Knowing the Senior Chief knew nothing about the system, I gave him enough rope to hang himself. His next act of defiance was trying to turn the department against me. He had negative discussions about me when he spoke to the troops out of my earshot. Once again little did he know that the individuals I trusted within the department came and told me what he was up to. All of this made my tour very challenging.

Part of understanding the system was our comradery and sport within the environment in which we were placed. System membership leads to discretion. While the actions taken may not be 100% moral or just, there's no one to challenge the system. Some of our actions we would not want to post on a network billboard. However, as long as they stay within the system's players, everything is okay. It's critical to be in alignment with the members of the system and the rules so you can see how some incidences just pass. if you are a novice and you think what's happening in the system is not correct and you try to expose the system, this act of calling out the system could have serious repercussions. I am not suggesting turning a blind eye to crimes within the system, but have to be careful with the system and its rules.

Take banana rat hunting, for example.

This was a pastime in Cuba. The Senior Chief didn't know I had built a good relationship with the Commanding Officer, the Staff Judge Advocate (SJA), and with all the other senior officers on the base. We would go out and hunt banana rats like men go golfing in the states to do deals! Banana rats were these super large rats that were nocturnal, and would come up into the housing area searching for water because it was hot and dry in Cuba. To kill these rats, you needed to shoot them with a double-aught buck-shot. The captain was a big skeet shooter, and he enjoyed going out to hunt these rats at night, but it was also team building, and this was building a strong relationship with the right people. One of the best things that ever happened was when we were out one night shooting rats and the Supply Officer with us, and the guys got a little overzealous. The rat ran between two rows of guys with shotguns. All we heard was what sounded like Armageddon.

"Guys, guys, I think I'm shot!" we heard.

We shot the Supply Corps officer in the legs! Blood was flying everywhere, and we called the ambulance to come to the magazine areas to get him. This could have been a career-ending event for the captain, the SJA, and myself. While sitting in the hospital, the captain asked me since I was the Ordnance Officer what should we do, and I told him we needed to report this immediately, but we needed to report it in such a way that it didn't sound like it was as bad as it was. I crafted up a message and sent it out that night, and the message was very encoded as we wrote it. We planned how we would address a board of inquiry once they found out the Commanding Officer had shot his Supply Officer on his base while hunting banana rats. The captain was reciting the answer he would give if the chairman of the board of inquiry asked him, did he check with his Staff Judge Advocate to see if it was okay to do what they were doing? His reply would be, "He was there, sir." The next question would be, what kind of an Ordnance officer do you have that would allow you guys to go out there with guns shooting on the base? And his reply would be, "He was there, too."

It was frustrating to think all our careers were in jeopardy for shooting banana rats and accidentally shooting a Supply Corps Officer. Luckily, none of us were ever questioned about what truly happened. However, the Staff Judge Advocate received a phone call from Washington D.C. asking him if was he the 04 (LCDR) who shot the 05 (CDR). Reluctantly, he said, "Yes, sir." The reply was, "It's about time someone shot a Supply Corps Officer." A very humorous ending to a very serious situation.

This encounter solidified the relationship between the captain, the SJA, and myself; the relationship that the Senior Chief knew nothing about. He did not understand how the system works. The Senior Chief thought he had a friend in the Executive Officer. This example was a clear perspective of someone having the misconception he had been invited into the boys club and he was not. Several times I tried to sit him down and explain to him that what he was seeing wasn't real, it was just an illusion that he thought he could trust the people around him. They didn't know him nor did they want to know him. All they wanted to do was use him, and he got used up. At the end of the day, the system is unforgiving. I saw here the application of Rule of the System #13 like I had with my ex-wife: *Cut ties quickly if someone is not aligned with your vision.* I should have fired this guy when I first saw him fishing.

The Executive Officer left him holding the bag and offered him no assistance whatsoever. He told the Senior Chief he didn't know what he was going to do if he were to be fired from my department, to find somewhere to go until the end of his tour. Fast forward and I had a friend who knew the Senior Chief and saw him years later, and the Senior Chief swore I ruined his career. He did not see his own mistakes nor did he see he was playing a game he knew nothing about. The moral of this story is to stay in your lane and understand the fight you're in at the time.

19 ~ THE ULTIMATE TEST OF THE SYSTEM

Aside from the Jamaicans, I had the worst department in my Navy career while in Cuba. My Senior Chief Petty Officer Bob was not a very bright man. He thought because we were the same age and color we must be equals. But I was an officer, and he was enlisted, which means we were not the same or equal. Because of this, he wanted to run the show, and when I put him in his place, he began to scheme behind my back. He got together with a few other people who had nothing else better to do and spread the word about what a horrible leader I was and how it was unfair. Accusations of reverse discrimination arose. You might wonder, what the heck is reverse discrimination? It's when one ethnicity is harder on the same ethnicity than others. The accusation was ludicrous. When you have a bunch of lazy people who don't understand the military system, they though it would be easy to have me removed from office. They wanted this badly so they could continue the carefree lifestyle they had become accustomed to before my arrival. They were not the intellectual, critical-thinking type of sailors you would want in your department.

The Senior Chief thought he could conspire with the Admin Officer and the Executive Officer (herein called the XO) to devise a plot to have me removed. The scheme was to complain about my leadership style to the Commanding Officer. This would be the move they thought would work, and the Commanding Officer would take action by removing me as the department head. The senior chief's motivation was retaliating against me because I was holding him accountable. Lucky for me I had the Jamaican division who knew how solid my leadership was and the good I was doing for the department. One could imagine what kind of uproar this stirred within the department. I had the Jamaican division whose average tenure was twenty years in the department. The Jamaicans had a great understanding of the history of the prior leaders, and they thought I was the best. I was shaken by these accusations initially; they had me questioning my leadership abilities. After my time in Philly and Georgia experiencing segregation, one would think the other African Americans would look after each other, but it was actually the opposite. Instead of being happy with a black leader, they were cut-throat about it.

I did a lot of soul-searching and reflection on my seventeen years of experience and my reputation and evaluations of sustained superior performance. All the things I did to get a commission as an officer hadn't changed, but now I couldn't lead a department? I went to my mentor John, the SJA, to talk about this circumstance. I went to a couple of other trusted officers to try to get some guidance on how to handle the situation. Of course, they did not want to participate. They were afraid of the Executive Officer. But my mentor provided great advice.

Unbeknownst to me, the plot to overthrow me was set in place by the Senior Chief, Admin Officer, and the XO. The major thing they overlooked was the seriousness of the accusations they were making, which were unfounded. This is a terrible, career-ending situation. In the Navy, they call it being relieved of your duties. This situation is invoked because either the individual is incompetent or they are a hazard to the well-being of the good order and discipline of the troops. I was neither.

What they did was wait until the Commanding Officer and the Staff Judge Advocate were off the island to enact their plot. They interviewed a few people in my department, and the senior chief was coaching them on what to say. They were told to say I was not following proper procedures when moving weapons and I was unfair when it related to recognizing top performers by only picking my favorites; all of which were lies. They put together what they thought was a strong case documenting everything they received from the sailor interviewed. The Admin Officer, because he was the best writer between the XO and the senior chief, thought he was the smartest thing since the beginning of time. He was, in fact, dumber than a box of rocks, just like the Executive Officer. They put this scheme in place, and they thought they had a foolproof plan. When the Commanding Officer returned to the command, they confronted him with this package on me.

"'Gunner Maxwell' is doing some horrible things within his department that warrant his removal."

They told him I was mistreating my people; I was unfair; I was ruthless and heartless; that I didn't care about the people; that I was giving them illegal orders. They had produced all sorts of crazy stuff. This report to the captain was so bad that when he read it, he thought the action was necessary. The captain never verified or discussed with me what he had received from the XO and Admin Officer.

My phone rang shortly after he read this report on a Friday afternoon.

"I've made the decision for the best interest of the Navy to remove you from my department."

That was it. He gave me no explanation. It was all based on the report he had read.

"I'm not sure what this is about," I said. "Am I the only one being held accountable here?"

"Yes," was his reply.

What more could I do? I was reassigned to the total quality leadership office, and that was where I was to stay until the end of my tour on base. Little did the XO and the Admin Officer know that I knew their system and I knew a better system. They did not know I operated from a strong base of rules that had kept me in the game to this point. My challenge was the XO and the Admin Officer thought they had their good old boy system in play. Both these guys were very ignorant. So the system they were playing in was archaic as opposed to an updated system I knew from evaluation and observation. Yet I couldn't be cocky about my position right from the get go because even if I knew their system was archaic, if you get enough like-minded people thinking the same way, their unsophisticated system could work. So never underestimate anyone and never feel superiority over anyone. You always look at the system for what it is.

So, like them, I rallied my team together. I called Washington D.C. and told him what happened. Then I talked to my friend, the Staff Judge Advocate, and the legal team. I did it the right way and contacted the right people for my defense.

If you have a negative system working around you, you cannot fix a negative system in a positive sense. Therefore you have to step out of the negative system and work in a positive system to find the right solution. If you try to operate in the negative system, you're going to consistently get negative answers, which are going to frustrate you. In recognizing the system, if it turns negative and you turn negative with it then you have a big ball of negativity.

What happens in this case is you're so caught up you don't see you're being sucked into a negative void. Once in that situation, I can assure you it is brutal to extract yourself. So what you have to do is stop, step out, and assess the container of the system you're in. You made it this far. You passed a fair amount of diverse trials to get here. It is imperative you make the needed corrections and then get back into the system aligned with your objectives and don't get consumed by the negativity around you. This will send you down a dark hole of no return. You need to step back for a critical view at what's going on.

In Guantanamo Bay, the negative environment I was working in was controlled by the XO. He continuously wanted to do combat with me. He had the power, and there's no way I could have won in that situation, and he knew it. The XO was an expert in the underhanded system. If I had gone head-to-head with him, just by his position and his rank, he would have won in a military environment. I had to step outside of the mousetrap of his negative system. I had to seek the friendship of the Staff Judge Advocate and the legal team, then I had to sit down and assess the root cause of what was going on in its entirety, and then finally put all of our heads together to formulate a plan and a solution.

What the captain did was wrong; he reacted without assessing the situation properly. He didn't have all this fact together. He took the word of the XO and the Admin Officer. Both had set out to try to destroy my career. When Monday came, the captain and the Staff Judge Advocate were talking about the situation. The Staff Judge Advocate told the Captain he had made a grave mistake. He let the XO and the Admin Officer lead him down a career-ending primrose path. The captain asked the SJA what he meant by that, and he told him that what the XO had done by having me removed was to serve his head on a silver platter to me.

That I would have him removed from command based on what happened and the actions he decided to exercise. The captain was shocked and dismayed at what he heard. He was extremely upset at the XO and the Admin Officer for the fabricated case against me.

On Wednesday, the captain called me to his office, and the XO and the Admin Officer were there in the room awaiting my arrival. He said to them he was unaware they had an axe to grind with me, and they were willing to go as far as they did to sabotage my career. The Commanding Officer reinstated me immediately as department head. He told the XO from that point forward he was no longer in my chain of command and that I reported directly to him (the CO). He proceeded to tell the XO that if he interfered with me again, it would end his career, and he told the same to the Admin Officer. Thank God for knowing the system and how to use it!

It is very critical when you're in challenging situations to stop and take a step outside of the situation so you can see clearly what's going on. When it looks like there is no way out, always seek outside counsel, and get someone else to give you their perspective. You need to have the ability to sit back and separate yourself from the situation. You need to look and see what is going on because the system properly understood will never fail you, but it can always be unforgiving if you don't show it respect.

You need to keep faith in the system, but most importantly, you have to understand the system you are dealing with at that time. You cannot get things mixed up in your head. You must stay focused on the situation at hand. You cannot let anyone or anything distract you in your quest to navigate through the system.

No matter what you do, never make it personal. If you let things get personal, this will cloud your judgement and steer you off course. it was amazing to see the face of the XO and the Admin Officer when they realized their plot had failed and failed miserably. Upon my return to my department, I called the Senior Chief into my office and told him I had lost faith and confidence in his ability to carry out my orders and relieved him of his duties and assignments. He was fired! The Senior Chief went running to the XO to tell him what I had done. He thought the XO would help him. The XO turned his back on the Senior Chief and said to him, "You're on your own." He did not support him. The Senior Chief did not know or understand the system. Because of this incident, the news got around the entire base on what the XO had done to me, so they pretty much had alienated themselves from the rest of the department heads. No one trusted the XO and Admin Officer anymore.

While there were moments during this situation when I thought my career was over, I stayed steadfast in my belief in my leadership abilities and leaned on the solid political relationships I had fostered in Cuba.

Regardless of internal strife, situations needed to be handled, and we were in the middle of a mass exodus of Cuban migrants and Haitian migrants to Guantanamo Bay. We had over 70,000 migrants on the base. The naval base was only designed to hold 7,000 military and civilians. My family and other dependents had to be evacuated off of the island for their safety. We could not afford an uprising from the migrants because there was no way to protect our families. Our only option would have been to commit a major atrocity by killing all the migrants. That was not a viable option for us to choose. The best option was to leave the military members on the station and send all the families off the island. Talk about poetic justice. The XO and the Admin Officer were excluded from all the future gatherings of other department heads while our families were evacuated. We all hung out together, we enjoyed each other, we kept each other's company since we had no family there on the island. This was a true testament of reaping what you sow in action. These two individuals (the XO and Admin Officer) with black hearts didn't mind destroying other people's careers just because they had the power to do so. In the end, they were the ones left holding the bag, and no one wanted to associate with them.

The system works as designed if you follow it with steadfast faith in your belief system, supported by the rules you have developed in your life. Systems, whether or not you have identified that way before this book, have been around since the beginning of time. The only variation in them is the players.

People will try and undermine your authority and take you down. You need your strong alliances, and even when it doesn't seem true, believe the system works. You have to know who's who in the zoo. You have to know good from evil and right from wrong. You have to build a strong allegiance with the right people, and you have to do what you do for the right reasons. Had I not had an understanding of how the system worked and what to expect from the system and how to use the system, my career would have been destroyed in Guantanamo Bay. This was a life-changing experience for me to see and know the system is real. There is a true adage that's been around forever: It is not *what* you know, but it's *who* you know. You have to understand that truth because we are humans and people work with people they like and people work against people they do not like. That's human nature.

Understand your trials and that you have to give and take to maintain the balance within the system. I learned a very valuable lesson from my time in Guantanamo Bay. I learned how circumstances dictated that I had to dig deep inside, and I had to figure out what were the problems and then I had to understand the root cause. I had to figure out the antidote, and how to insert a correction without having it blow up in my face. It's been over twenty-five years, and I'm still best friends with the Staff Judge Advocate, who is now a partner in a law firm in Tampa, Florida. He continues to do wonderful things and is still a wonderful person.

20 ~ TOMAHAWK CRUISE MISSILE TRAINING PROGRAM

The Navy has a performance rating system called fitness reports that are akin to report cards in high school. The fitness reports have alphabet rating grades, A's, B's, C's, and D's. To receive anything other than "A" is a kiss of death to one's career. Surviving Guantanamo Bay with all A's on my fitness report and an early promotion mark was an outstanding challenge and a great way to finish up such an intense tour. Gitmo was the toughest duty assignment I ever endured. Because of keeping the faith and believing in the system, I survived unscathed. That duty station challenged every moral fiber in me, and it challenged my leadership abilities, my character, and my ethics. I passed the life test with flying colors. Remember, life gives the test first and then the lesson. What I did know was I could not bring the negative experience of Cuba with me to my next assignment. All I could do is look back to prevent the circumstances of doing the same thing over again.

My next Detailing Officer suggested I take a sea-going assignment. At this point in my life, Gitmo was so challenging there was no way I could have been assigned to a ship right after this tour. Shipboard duties are very challenging in and of themselves. My

169

Detailing Officer and I had a very good relationship; he understood where I was at as far as pushing my limits mentally.

He sent me to the weapons training group command instead as the officer-in-charge of the Tomahawk Cruise Missile Training Program. This new job was different and rewarding. Our mission was to train all ships and submarines on the proper use, handling, and launching of the tomahawk cruise missile, a very important job.

The location was in beautiful San Diego, right back where I started. The detailer kept his promise on getting me back to San Diego. I needed to get back to San Diego because we had established a home there and the kids had initiated school in that area. My goal was to have my kids finish school in the same location where they started.

Interestingly, the team I had in my new duty assignment in the weapons training group was exactly 180 degrees different from the team I had in Guantanamo Bay. I now had the sharpest, smartest, professional sailors the Navy could offer. I went from one perspective to the absolute opposite overnight. My right-hand man would always tell me to relax in my office and he would take care of everything in the organization. This was a far cry away from the Senior Chief Petty Officer I had to fire in Gitmo. I remember a time during this tour when I was informed at 3:00 pm that three-star Vice Admiral Tracy was coming the next morning to inspect my spaces. She wanted to know more about the work I was performing. My team could handle last-minute inspections because they were high-quality Petty Officers and organized. My Senior Chief told me not to worry; he had everything under control.

The next morning, I showed up at my office, and I had a very well-prepared brief laid out on my desk ready to go for the Vice Admiral. When Vice Admiral Tracy showed up, I introduced her to the team and gave her the brief. She said it was one of the best briefs she had ever heard. Vice Admiral Tracy was one of the first females in the Navy to achieve the rank of three-star admiral. She was a very impressive individual. It was an honor and privilege to have her come inspect my command.

I was trying to mask my total disbelief in the superior support I received from my staff.

I thought to myself how just months earlier I was in a situation where I was questioning my worth to the United States Navy, and here I sat now with an outstanding team of folks who did an amazing job for me. Working at this new command clarified the intent of some sailors. GITMO was a command where sailors hid when they didn't want to participate in positive functions. Most sailors take the GITMO job knowing they have reached the end of their career growth. I learned that after the assignment there in GITMO. This was a testament for me and my life to realize that sometimes circumstances dictate the outcome of everything.

My new job in San Diego was wonderful, and I had a great crew of sailors. We visited bases in Newport, Rhode Island and other locations. During our off time there, we did some sightseeing of the old mansions and enjoyed the great seafood in Rhode Island. The team did so well with the admiral's visit that I took everyone out to breakfast to show my appreciation for their hard work, dedication, and commitment. I got to know them more on a personal basis. I invited them to my home for a big pool party and BBQ.

I did have some challenges in my new job, but they were cupcakes in comparison to my previous job. I had a young lady who wanted to be the first female to serve on a submarine. At the time, the Navy did not have any females serving on submarines. She was an individual who had been given every promotion without testing for the advancement. She was the National City Woman of the year, sailor of the year, and so on. She was a political hound dog, and any opportunity that would get her recognition, she went for it. It was all about her. Her focus was completely off-balance and driven in the wrong direction, which caused her career to suffer immensely after she went from the number one E6 to be promoted to E7.

Because of her lack of experience that she should have gained by working hard and earning her promotions, she did not make the transition to E7 very well. I had twenty-six Chief Petty Officers working for me. Because of her misaligned career focus, she became number twenty-six out of twenty-six, at the bottom of the barrel of chiefs that worked for me. Her attitude ruined her career. She was an individual who did not understand what systems were about and how to operate in the systems. This individual was fooled by the system. She did not adjust to the changing environments as she moved up the levels of the system. So, at her next level she tried to use her beginning-level antics and it didn't work for her. She had not developed and established her rules by which she could best operated in the system. Therefore, she was inconsistent and inefficient.

She was completely consumed by herself. This is one of the dangers of not understanding the system. You have to recognize the give and take that is associated with the system. It's not going to always play in your favor immediately, but you can't run at the first sign of trouble or start blaming other for your faults when things don't go your way.

This situation with this female sailor was an educational experience. Her former boss, who became one of my best friends, set her up for failure. When he had the chance to correct her, he would let her get away with all types of things. She had been coddled throughout her career. Then along comes Mr. accountable (that's me). I held her accountable for her actions and didn't allow her to take credit for things she didn't deserve. Back then in the Navy, sexual harassment was fairly new or just beginning to take hold. A lot of senior officers were afraid to be in an office with a female with the office door closed. I would not have a female in my office with the door closed. Too many careers were ended by sexual harassment accusations.

21 ~ USS STETHEM DD-63

Two years passed and my tour in San Diego ended. Now I was being assigned back to a ship. I had regained my composure from Cuba and was mentally prepared to serve on board a warship. Right before I transferred, Muammar Gaddafi in Libya violated some trade agreements at the same time as the Monica Lewinsky scandal was going on with President Bill Clinton. The United States fired thirteen Tomahawk cruise missiles at Libya. My team was responsible for doing the damage assessment to find out how effective the accuracy of the weapons were at the targets. These events were going on in the world. We watched the political maneuvering and diversion that controlled what we watched on TV. I was very excited to be a part of this world event.

At one point, I was under the belief that trouble followed me. From the mass exodus of migrants in Cuba to now launching missiles at Libya, my life was right out of a movie. But even though there was a lot going on, none of it affected me being transferred to the USS Stethem DD-63. This new ship was an advanced technology warship. My new job was as the Systems Test Officer (STO). This had to be the coolest job in the Navy. I had the chance to employ tactics and different ways on how to fight, which weapons to deploy, and which missiles to Launch.

One situation in the Persian Gulf was very similar to the Kinkaid situation. The difference was we were employing troops to board an unflagged cargo ship. To do this type of operation in the northern Persian Gulf was very dangerous. What you didn't know was who was on that ship or what weapons they had. So you had to use the ship we were on as a barrier and launch our men from the opposite side. We won't use our ship's guns as protection while our men row in small boats to board that ship's platform.

The Officer of the Deck should have been someone who had experience, normally a lieutenant, but the one we had wasn't experienced enough to do the assignment. He wanted to launch our men without cover. I would not let that happen as a Conning Officer (the Conning Officer is the ship's driver). We got our men over to the ship, boarded it and inspected it, and we brought them back safe. After the event, the lieutenant came to me and said I had better not question his orders ever again. I told him if he came within another three inches of me, I would knock his head off, and that I would never put our men in harm's way ever again.

When he realized he was making a huge mistake, he backed down, and later he and I became friends. During the event, everything was very intense and serious.

When you go on deployment on a U.S. Navy vessel, your only lifeline is that ship, so you do everything in your power to protect the ship and the crew. As officers on board, that is our job to do at all costs. There's no time for mistakes because mistakes cost lives. After this event had happened and I had time to think about it, I was very proud of myself for the decisions I made and the risk I was not willing to take with our men. The Officer of the Deck was inexperienced and did not fully understand the harm he was about to do the men who were on the small boat we had launched to board the hostile vessel. I was not going to have a Kinkaid moment ever again. I called my wife and told her about the incident. She just laughed at me slightly and said the reason why I did what I did was to make up for the events on board USS Kinkaid several years earlier. I already knew the truth to her statement. I learn from my mistakes, and I also learned all the systems operated on board the new ship. I was about the same age as the Commanding Officer, and he had built trust in me so he and I could have off-the-record conversations about life and family. Commanding Officer of a naval ship is probably the loneliest job in the world. It's not like you can be open with very many individuals. You have to present the face of wisdom, courage, and intelligence all the time. No one gets to see the real person. It's a job I never had, but I can only imagine the level of responsibility every day, especially in a wartime scenario.

We had a great captain. He was a good man, and he understood the crew very well, unlike the captain aboard the Kinkaid, who was completely out of touch with the crew. This guy was dialed completely in with everyone on board. As a matter of fact, he and I are still friends to this day.

The Executive Officer that we had on board this ship was good, but he was different. He reminded me of the last kid picked on a baseball team. He was looking for a friend. When we were in Australia, he called me to a stateroom and told me he wanted to go out on the town with me. Mind you, I like to pick and choose who I went out on the town with when overseas, but because he was an Executive Officer, I couldn't say no. This had to be the most boring night of my life. The things he wanted to do, like go to gentlemen's clubs and hang out in seedy bars, I had no interest in doing. All I could do this entire night was try to see things that interested me or to try to make the best out of a bad situation. The importance of understanding the system was I could not let him know I was not having a good time because I needed him as an ally on board the ship. It is critical that sometimes you cannot show your hand. If you know you need someone who has control within your system but you don't care for them, it's time to put on a happy face and suck it up. You cannot show reality. As you can see, now that I had my solid list of the Rules of the System, I could accentuate and expand on them, elevating me to a higher level of operating.

So I put up with him for the night. Sometimes working in the system, you can't let anything get under your skin. You have to roll with the punches and look at the greater good. Look at the bigger picture, look at the worth and value and what it is that you're doing.

One day while I was the Command Duty Officer, the Executive Officer called me up and told me he and the captain wanted me to go sailing with them on the Australian Captain's sailboat. I informed him I had duty, and his reply was, "I didn't ask you that. Meet me at the Quarterdeck." I followed his orders. I had the best time of my life. I got to sail a thirty-five-foot sailboat in the Sydney Harbor, in front of the Sydney Amphitheater. It was a dream come true. I thought about the night he asked me out, and had I been a real jerk, I never would have got the opportunity I had that day. This was not about friends, but there were benefits by not resisting. I didn't predict this wonderful outcome from being available to a decision maker. He could have made my career easy or hard. I stomached my initial feelings and it worked out. Sometimes you have to tolerate situations because you are not clear about the whys.

While I was on board the USS Stethem, we were deployed with the same ship I was deployed with on board the Kinkaid—the USS Rentz. In the northern Persian Gulf, the USS Rentz

Executive Officer and Squadron Officer decided to take one of the helicopters out on an evening flight. Unfortunately for them, during liftoff the back wheel of the helicopter was caught in the nets surrounding the flight deck. This caused the helicopter to topple over like a toy and land in the water of the Persian Gulf. The crew was able to escape because there was only about sixty feet of water. Because I was new on board the ship, when they were briefing the recovery of the helicopter, this event took place right outside my stateroom in the wardroom. I decided to go over and listen to what was going on, not that I had any involvement with it, but I thought I might as well listen. After they finished briefing the event, I went back to my stateroom. Shortly after that, I received a phone call from the Executive Officer who instructed me to go over to the recovery ship and take over tactical command for our captain. The recovery ship was a United States Navy Ship, which is the designation given to non-commissioned ships that are property of the United States Navy, meaning it was not a warship. Therefore, because this was a warship incident in hostile waters, the warship had tactical control. It was 11:00 p.m. and dark. The conditions were sea state about three or four, which means it was somewhat choppy. I was cold and I was tired. Like a good sailor, I went over to the recovery vessel, which was led by a civilian captain. This guy cussed me out from the time I stepped on board his ship until the time I left. I had to let him know several times that my captain was the on-site commander in charge of the recovery operations and it didn't matter that this was his ship. Three days later, we were able to recover the helicopter from the bottom of the ocean.

When I returned on board USS Stethem, I realized I how after twenty-two years in the Navy, it wasn't fun for me anymore. When we reached Bahrain, I called my wife and I told her I was thinking about throwing in the towel. I was ready to retire. She said to me she had been waiting for this phone call for several years now. I could not get back to my stateroom fast enough to put in my resignation papers. We had a successful Westpac return home with no incidents in six months as planned.

22 ~ A Naval Career in Retrospect

I had been through the fire with various challenging conditions in the Navy. At this point in my life, from all the learning and conditioning I experienced from my Philly roots to the taste of Georgia and through my Naval experience, I had my Rules of the System. The question was whether I would have the fortitude to use my knowledge to implement them. I was beaten up a bit and I had put up a thick wall around me, but I mastered my understanding of the strength of the players in the system. I had developed and mastered critical awareness to bring into real-world situations. I was now exposed to how the system worked and could recognize when the systems are in play, even in romantic relationships.

This is a crossroads for you once you have taken on conditions foreign to you and come out stronger on the other side. You have seen people behaving poorly and disrespecting the system, and how it can affect your life. You will continue to be tested now because you haven't given up. The key is to remain focused on your core objectives. You may not know yet how to recognize what you will need in the system you working or living in at this time, but do not let it throw you off course to the bigger purpose of your mission. You might not recognize the players right away, but give it time and it will unveil itself. As soon as you identify your bigger purpose, stay with it steadfastly. False distractions or illusions will enter the picture to entice you to think differently than the true course you are on. At this point in the knowledge base, with not yet understanding the bigger perspective, circumstances can turn on you. Fallout from going off course is where you have the hard cold lesson that the system is unforgiving because it doesn't care about your individual needs or desires; it's only purpose is to be part of a time and motion continuum.

At this stage, having weathered significant career and personal growth, should you be steadfast, you will be given the chance to course-correct and make the right choices. If, at this point, you make a wrong choice, you must quickly get back into alignment with either your original desires or find a new system to orchestrate your desires within. Efficiency and swift thinking is critical because time is not on your side. You can make corrections along the way, but you have to realize when a mistake has occurred; pride or ignorance must not get in the way, especially when you are dealing with super-smart individuals who understand the system and may not have your best interests at heart, or really ignorant players in the system who are persistent in effecting your demise. I can't insist upon this Rule of the System enough: *Constantly survey the environment to ensure every day you see where you are at.*

I had to go through a wide, sweeping range of complicated and challenging career and personal experiences to know I had what it takes to make the long haul to my greater purpose. Knowing my objectives and continually focusing on what I had to do to entertain them always took precedence. To ascend to the next level of your life, strong support from your life partner is essential. You cannot have someone around you questioning your every move, especially if they do not understand your bigger plan. They need to unwaveringly stand by the value you bring to a situation while you are in the thick of unfortunate, and in my case, sometimes disastrous events. A person in your life wasting your time because you have to worry about their behavior is dead weight and will pull you down.

You need confidence in your course of action at every turn as you go for bigger recognition, titles, money, or a greater level of accomplishment, and need to have a plan B in your pocket ready to go at all times. Being cool and sexy is not enough to reach for the heights of success I hope for you to obtain. Never be too demanding. Sure, we all want to put on a tailored suit, drive a Porsche, and vacation in the Bahamas, but these side perks were never what drove me to my greater purpose of autonomy and connection with a message to inspire and serve others. My purpose had depth and weight and required an unwavering stance. You must be driven to go on with the life mission you choose or do yourself a favor and give it up. The trials and tests as you go up the ladder of systems, encountering people who are more cunning and vicious, are not for the weak of fortitude. A lukewarm perspective will knock you out of the running.

People who think they understand the system but cannot give up their past ways fail every time. Go back to my suggestion of identifying the messages given to you in the system of your childhood. Ask yourself why you are still identifying with an environment you left. Then take my list of the Rules of the System and shape the life you truly desire.

People exist on this earth clueless about their surroundings. A deeper understanding of the system they are in is not important to them because they're happy with where they are, and that's okay. Not everyone was meant to be a president or a leader; we need the janitors, the dishwashers, and the window washers. These levels of individuals are needed critically to be a part of the system; everyone has a role. As you navigate through life, you need to know what role everyone plays, the little and big players. I don't want to make life sound like some cloak and dagger affair, but it's the world we live in no matter what your background is or your cultural upbringing. We all deal with systems at different levels, and if you don't know how to identify and navigate them, you can be brought to your knees.

You could decide you are where you need to be already, work thirty years, retire, and wait for social security. However, I'd venture to say, if you are reading this book, you have a desire for higher life objectives. You are not dialing in your life satisfactorily. Or you have and you are sick and tired of not achieving your highest self and want to take a stab at it now. I chose to make the Navy a career. My choice was to either finish my career as an officer or as the most senior enlisted person as I could be, nothing in between. Whatever your personal mission, you will have to tactfully navigate the systems surrounding you to see success.

At this point, you should have learned some discernment of the players in your system. You can spot who are your allies. You will also understand from observation that Bob is a strong player, and Sally is the decision-maker. Then you will know that Jim is the perpetrator. You can't waste time with the perpetrator. When you are ready to start playing, you have to decide how aggressive you are going to be because there are only two choices: Either you win or you lose. Winning means winning big. For me, losing meant my Navy career was over. At all times, when dealing with the perpetrator, do not get consumed by their actions. Always be kind, courteous, disarming and unassuming; feed them minimal stuff to keep them pacified. You never let them know your intentions. You are basically deceptive, but that is part of survival.

It's also not important to always win in certain conflicts or disagreements. Let others win. For example, in a competitive environment, it may not be your turn, but you are on the list to win eventually. If you wait, then on next go around you'll get the promotion or job you were seeking. You have to recognize and play in the environment. At this point, you cannot challenge it; you cannot challenge the players; you just have to suck it up and deal with it. You can't give up or be resentful because if you do, that knocks you out as a contender. You won't get another shot. Always remember the system is unforgiving.

You will receive recognition, promotions, and be considered a mentor or a go-to person when you operate from the foundation you created. You are now removed from a lot of the nonsense and people only come to you with positive discernments. Some people tend to think because you are easy-going you must be soft or weak, and that can be a huge mistake on their part. Don't let people with bravado sway you into thinking you need to be like them to get ahead and achieve goals. Anyone who ever saw me in that way was surprised by the lion that showed up. I've always acted like the silent ninja who chops you into pieces while you sleep. You don't have to be the loud voice in the room. Being the loud voice in most cases will show your cards and will show your intentions, and this will definitely end your battle quickly.

In the collision at sea, I lost faith in the overarching system I thought I believed in; this was a classic example of misreading the tea leaves. I thought prior to becoming an officer that all officers were aboveboard, honest, and decent individuals. During the collision, I realized there were a lot of unethical people that wore officers' uniforms. After the incident, we had to see a psychiatrist to ensure that we're still capable of carrying out the Navy's mission. I told him I could give a crap about this system. I was done, over and out. I was affected by the lack of control I had in that situation and the best action I could take was to remove myself from the Navy. The psychiatrist saw I had an ability to get back in and fight. He recommended to the commanding officer that I get back on board the ship. I couldn't see at the time how I had a bright future ahead of me. This situation was an incredible test of my internal fortitude and my ability to stay in the system. I just had to get over that hurdle. Sometimes you have to trust outside influences that can see what you cannot to keep you in the system. Stay open-minded, and don't be so restrictive in your decision making. I could not let one extremely bad situation cloud my understanding of how the system was working; I had been chosen, so I had to fight the fight. I am glad he pushed me to return because I needed to get back in it and learn to move forward.

Don't ever rest on your laurels. Just because you are accepted into a more refined club, or a higher stature, you must still constantly surveil the environment to ensure you don't have blinders on or get complacent. When I was stationed in Cuba, the system did not see color, but I saw I had a department that was three-quarters black American sailors and one smaller division of Jamaicans. I knew from my past experiences in environments like Philly and Georgia that the American black sailors had the potential to work together to thrive, but they didn't. The Jamaicans were different. They saw the opportunity before them in this little world we had on the base with its own beach, BBQ, and fishing area. Our area was exclusive to only people who worked in my department. A majority of the sailors who worked for me got caught up in the backbiting and senseless foolishness in my division caused by the senior enlisted person who was a Senior Chief Petty Officer. He had hopes of destroying me because he had a problem—we were not equals even though we were the same age and color. I was an officer and he was enlisted. So, he joined with the other rogue officers to ostracize me. No group of officers are going to side with an enlisted officer, although they used him as an inside man.

He had no idea he was being used by their system to get back at an old perceived injustice. He was trying to get involved despite my warnings of telling him he was out of his league. He continued with expectations of a happy ending. He thought if he joined up with them in destroying me, he would get rewarded for it. I warned him his decisions were all wrong. I even tried to explain to him how the system works, but he was one of those super-slick smart guys who couldn't hear anything I said because he knew better. I told him clearly to not play because the system is unforgiving. He was, of course, defeated in his efforts when I went into a system above him to prove allegations against me as erroneous. I have seen the system leave a lot of people in the dust, jeopardizing their families and careers, and swallow the connivers and manipulators who have no clue what they have attempted to engineer for their own benefit. I have seen countless stories end badly.

Good people tend to cruise along in the system fine, but you also need a brash awareness that there are systems in the first place. When I understood this life framework, I was able to orchestrate my life more effectively on a higher level. You don't have to be a jerk, but you need to be steadfast. More can be gained with a spoonful of sugar than salt—this is an old saying from my grandma. People will gravitate to you better than those who crash around like a bull in a china shop.

While operating in the system and in life, you should always have a plan A and plan B in place. Although you may only desire plan A fully in your heart, you always have to think through both plans with the possibility of a course correction. Questions you have to constantly ask yourself while operating in the system include the following: What happens if this doesn't work? What happens if it doesn't work as well but still works? You have to be able to adjust and re-prioritize and set goals as you move along.

You have to think all scenarios all the way through. You have to think about the home run before you swing the bat. The highly successful winners start with the end in mind. This is so critical because if you don't know what your end objective is or how to get there, including all the roadblocks, you're just wandering in the wilderness. Sometimes the end objective may not be the perfect ending, but at least you have a perfect objective.

These are some very critical words I'm about to say: When you're in the system and it fails you, don't try to fix it. Sometimes it's best just to walk away. If I had fought the system with all sorts of rationality, I would have ended up not having an opportunity to continue and get into that psychiatrist's office. I did not churn myself into the ground trying to prove my innocence and position. I knew what was done was done with the collision and accepted the outcome.

I quickly learned as an officer how the system I used when I was enlisted was now different. I needed to be more strategic, thoughtful, and more intellectual. I was dealing with very smart people now who came from solid educational backgrounds. You must have the ability to change as an environment changes. Be open to learning, and be receptive and once again, you must put your pride on the shelf.

Eventually, you may be tasked with creating or making your own system. You can do so by implementing all the rules you have established that have guaranteed success. You can be the master of your craft or the captain of your ship. How you go through this next phase determines if you make it to the master's program of life.

After twenty-two years in the U.S. Navy, my life was destined to become even more interesting as I navigated new systems in both the private and public sectors, which you'll read about in the third part of this book.

PART III

Forging New Paths in the Private and Public Sectors

23 ~ INTO THE PRIVATE SECTOR

My day of awareness and maturing in the system was during my tour as the Ordnance Officer in Guantanamo Bay, Cuba. I learned very valuable lessons during that stage in my life. Rule of the System # 10 was continuously in play: *Be discerning about whom you trust with your ambitions.* Had it not been for a strong marriage, a solid financial footing, education, and understanding how what you see is not always the truth, I would have never made it to retiring from the Navy and building a business. I was embarking on the creation of my own system in which I could be the master controller.

Leaving the Navy and going back into society as a civilian was upon me. I had to implement everything I learned for the last four decades in the real world. I was no longer operating in the box of the military. No matter what your rank was, you have to operate in your authority box. This can be akin to being in one career your whole life and then leaving for a completely different career. You may think there are no similarities or parallels, but where they exist is in the Rules of the System you have established and developed for yourself. Understanding and playing in the system is not for the faint of heart. It's not for the uneducated. And it's certainly not for the unknowing or the unwilling.

Now I could see the social divide between the haves and the have-nots. The have-nots tend to believe in a storybook world about how life is supposed to be, not the real world. In the storybook world, everything is fair, everything is honest, and everything is beautiful. Everyone loves each other and everyone does all the things one thinks are right. That's not reality. What world do you live in? In order to achieve autonomy in your life, and build your own system, you need to be deeply aware of reality. This comes from understanding all the environments that have crossed your path. They are all there to teach you if you are open and willing to take the steps to learn, and follow the Rules of the System.

In order to acquire all you desire, you need to stick with the fundamental fact that in life there are rules to follow. You have a choice in what set of rules you adhere to. I had my set of Rules of the System I had developed though my life laid out in the opening of this book. At this juncture, you should be mature with understanding what the rules are to apply to the system you are in, be they mine or a version of your own creation. You have to make very clear choices as to how you live in the system, especially when it comes to mastering an environment in which you are in charge. Being the boss is not for everyone. Some individuals are happy going along to get along, working for thirty years in a widget factory on the widget line and never moving up. That's okay, but if you have the desire to own the widget factory, then there are some *additional guidelines to the System* that must be implemented and applied for your success in business, including the following:

- Be very aware of who the individuals are that have the ear of leadership because they can make or break your progress.
- Know your support system internally and externally.
- Don't be afraid to change direction or location.

- Vet and deal only with trusted companies. Continue to stay close to your circle, which should be extremely small.
- Never put yourself in a compromising situation, and if you do, keep a cool head in order to get out. Trust you will persevere.

When I became a business owner of a nationwide company, I learned through trial and error to apply the above rules outside the military where I had operated for twenty-two years. You have companies that think everything is fair and honest. You have companies that read the guerilla marketing book and try to apply those tactics to manage their business. But in either case, you see these businesses failing or operating below standards. What I've learned is that successful businesses understand the systems that surround them. They understand how to use the network, and they stay aware of their surroundings.

When you look at our world and you look at the social divide, that gap is getting wider. To the point, if you try to sit down and talk to someone who does not understand how the system works, they will think you are above yourself. And you cannot convince them to see reality.

One of the most critical aspects in this system to survive are Rules of the System #11 and #12: *Don't take anything personally. This is a waste of your time* and *There will be haters, don't let them get you caught up in their world.*

When I was in the military it was harder to avoid these folks, but as a business owner, I had the power to hire, fire, and do what was necessary to protect the livelihood of myself, my family, and my employees. Despite how personal it may seem, you always must look for the greater good for you, and you must understand the merits of what's in front of you. The blame game doesn't work.

You must know who's a friend and who's a foe. It doesn't mean you can't do business with a foe, but you do have to have know-how because they have a system too. I've found in life that when you deviate from the strict Rules of the System, you will suffer trouble and loss.

There are examples around this every day. Like the San Francisco 49ers quarterback who tried to change the NFL system, but the system got rid of him. Like the president of the United States who didn't want to abide by the Rules of the System despite how ugly things looked, and the system tarnished his record. I've met so many people who felt they were not given a fair shake. When you ask them if they identified and abided by the rules of the system they were in, they would admit they strayed from what was expected of them. They attempted to force change. In whatever system you are in, whether forced or self-identified, you will know when it's time to make changes. The universe will make it so uncomfortable for you that you will have no choice but to leave the environment. When you are not happy in a situation, don't stay in denial and try to make it work. The world has better plans for you. Trust in the process and do your part by aligning yourself with what you want. The rest will be history. I've also learned that adversity is there to test you. Adversity is not the enemy; it's there to make you better and to humble you.

Keep in mind, the system is not negative or positive. It's the life platform you must live by in your daily life to achieve your goals and desires. Later in life I brought church into my world, where there are also systems to abide by. No environment is off-limits to the system. I've witnessed greatness in the church I attend. The pastor is an awesome human being who knows many of the systems well (political, business, and so on). Our church is one of the wealthiest churches in San Diego County. Why? The foundation of the church is built on a strong internal and external system. The pastor has assimilated with the local San Diego political leadership and has built a strong internal team of individuals who support his efforts. The ones who do not are quietly overlooked and placed in positions with little to no responsibility. Better yet, some who are not educated enough to know about the system are not educated any further. What amazes me the most about this situation is how the church is an all-volunteer organization. It takes great leadership to accomplish this feat. Understanding and observing there are systems even in places of faith was the final assurance to me that my way of operating has developed over the decades is right on the mark. I gained strength to create a business that can reach goals even beyond my wildest imaginings. Life remains exciting and continuously unfolding when you have faith in the systems.

24 ~ A CAREER IN DEFENSE

I put in my papers while deployed, but everything went into action once we returned to San Diego. My resignation was my retirement papers, and it was so funny because the first time I submitted them, they were denied. Due to the needs of the Navy, they couldn't afford to let me retire at the time I requested. I had to wait a few months and request again, and they shot it down yet again. I had one last trick in my tool bag, and it was I knowing that if I went on limited duty, they would have no choice but to release me from the ship. This tactic almost blew up in my face because I had surgery on my foot, which put me in a limited duty status. I learned that the Executive Officer of the ship could cancel limited duty status, and he did, I had no idea he had so much power. At his level, he shut down my request for retirement, overruling a scenario I was unaware he had the power to orchestrate. A valuable lesson to learn while maneuvering through a system I thought I controlled.

I had to change my tactics, so I cornered the doctor and told her I served my country for twenty-two years and I was ready to go home. I told her I would not settle for denial. I put the ownership on her to go above the ship's Executive Officer. She was able to get the Commanding Officer of the hospital to overrule the Executive

Officer on the ship. I was placed on limited duty, and I retired after twenty-two years of wonderful service in the Navy.

Finally, I was able to get off the ship, and once off the ship my future was in my hands. My detailer still insisted I pull my papers and stay in the Navy for thirty years. I did contemplate this, but my oldest daughter was entering high school, and I felt I needed to be home a little more. So I refused to pull my papers. They sent me over to the Aegis Training and Readiness command to wait until my retirement was finalized. I was the Division Officer for information assurance, which today we call cybersecurity. I had no idea I was being set up for the future, but it was being dropped in my lap. Again, staying compliant but also assertive was what I learned in the system.

My entry into the defense industry came through this position. Another lieutenant had a connection for me, so I set up an interview. I did, and within a couple of days, he called me up for an interview. I was looking for a job at the same time a job was looking for me. I was also finishing up my graduate degree in computer information systems. I was transitioning out of the Navy, job hunting, and finishing up my master's degree all at the same time. The Master of Science in Computer Information Systems (MSCIS) became the obvious choice because in the industry there was an issue between the computer lay person and the computer geeks. A major communications challenge existed. The MSCIS individual was more of a translator from geek to common language about computer systems.

In my first week at the new job, they sent me and a couple other teammates to a company for a partnering opportunity. I walked in the door and met this one guy named Bill Gerhardt, and Bill starts talking to me with all the typical introductions, and the next guy I met was George. George and I had served together when I was an officer in charge of Tomahawk missile training. The first comment out of George's mouth was, "Hey man, are they treating you all right?" I was so new in the transition I had no way of knowing how to answer George, so I just said, "For now everything is fine." George said to me, "I want you over here in this company with me because I know how you are." He told me he was getting a promotion to vice president, and he wanted to bring me in as his deputy director of operations. He first had to hire me on as a program manager and then I would shortly get promoted to the deputy director of operations.

Everything is about timing. Because I was so new to the transition, it made sense for me to learn more about the industry rather than to jump into something I didn't know. So after about a year, I made the transition to his company, which we can call Company A. The company I was leaving, Company B, had a philosophy that kept individuals unaware of how the government contracting system worked. They treated individuals as if the workers were McDonald's employees, not affording them the information about how the business ran. I was so new to the industry; I didn't know any better. In the system, experience is the best teacher. As smart and intelligent an individual I thought I was, this was a new beginning for me. My experience assisted with the transition, but I also knew that the playing field was different than the military.

During that year, I finished my master's degree a year to the day George called me up and said, "Are you ready to come over?" Being aware caused me to utilize Rule of the System #3: *Constantly survey the environment to ensure every day you see where you are at.* I had been out of the Navy now for about a year and Company B was excited about me returning with a higher degree, not knowing George had made me an offer. I took George's offer. Company B was praising me and telling me they saw the future with me and their company, and at the same time I was handing them my resignation because I was going to move over to George's company.

Company B was furious when they found out what my plan was. I tried to explain to them I enjoyed their company and they would have a friend and another company as opposed to a competitor. The local leaders in San Diego did not want to hear that. So he made the transition somewhat ugly and uncomfortable. I made the move anyway, invoking Rule of the System # 13: *Cut ties quickly if someone is not aligned with your vision.*

George kept his promise hired me as a program manager and within a month I was offered the deputy director of operations position. A gentleman by the name of Clyde was going to get promoted to director of operations. Clyde was a retired Navy Captain, and very experienced both as a senior leader in the military and in the industry for several years. When Clyde said to me, "Why don't you take the director of operations spot, and I'll be your deputy," his rationale was I had a bright future ahead of me, and he was looking only to work for a few more years and retire once again for good. It is important to have a mentor in any new system, and Clyde became mine. I was very lucky to have a mentor like him to help me navigate through a new and different level of the system and the changes in my life.

The benefit here at the new company was they taught me all the inner workings of the business. I learned about writing proposals. I learned about teaming up with other companies. I learned about pricing, and I understood how contracts worked. Everything was going along fine. I was doing well as the Director of Operations with more than fifty people working for me in the San Diego area. Life was good. My government customer and I had a great relationship. I was a hard worker, and she was somewhat lazy. But as a team it worked out well. One day when I was somewhat fed up with her lazy approach to things, I had a list that was about two pages to talk to her about—things we needed to bring into focus and do a better job at completing. She said to me, "Allen, before you get into this with me, you need to understand I am quitting my job."

When she said that, my heart sank in my chest because she was the financial person for me. She was the government individual who paid the bills for my employment. I was speechless. So I sat there for a few minutes trying to collect my thoughts, my mind was racing at a million miles per hour, and all I could think about was losing my job. A few days passed by, and I went to speak to her boss, who was a Navy Captain, and asked what was his thoughts were on the situation. He said to me, "Allen, we know you were the behind-the-scenes guy making everything happen, so why don't you just come into the government and move into her position." I was experiencing an additional aspect of the rules of the system: *Be very aware of who the individuals are that have the ear of leadership because they can make or break your progress.*

I was excited, because this was playing right into my hand. It was perfect. The transition process took four months and then I was a government employee.

25 ~ GPS: THE PULSE OF NEW TECHNOLOGY

My new government position was as a GPS User Equipment Assistant Program Manager. I was responsible for all GPS equipment that went on board all naval ships, airplanes, and submarines. During the Clinton administration, there was a Commerce Secretary named Ron Brown whose airplane crashed into the side of a mountain overseas. What was learned from the crash was how all military airplanes, ships and submarines could not navigate without GPS. His plane became disoriented because they had no means of knowing their exact position. President Bill Clinton enacted an edict that said all U.S. military airplanes, ships and submarines would have GPS installed. My job was to ensure that this happened. The initial effort to install GPS on military platforms was a huge undertaking, and it took years to install all of this equipment.

I joined the team in October, 1998 and the completion of the installation was in 2005. We learned after the installation was finally completed that there needed to be a technical refresh on all of the equipment. This caused a long-term continuation of support in the installation of this equipment. President Clinton opened up the GPS accuracy to the civilian population. By doing so, this exposed a level of accuracy equal to the military. Military

GPS accuracy must be more accurate than civilian equipment. Before we could do a technical refresh on the equipment already installed, we had to develop a new GPS signal code that was more accurate than what was being used by civilians.

My first few weeks were an acclimation period for my new environment. I thought initially that most of the people I was working with had their stuff together as I encountered as an Officer in my various positions of military leadership. I was surrounded by people who, at one point in time, were hot stuff, but the bureaucratic system the government breeds beat them down. Most people gave up and went to the ROAD program. In the military, we call this Retired On Active Duty. I had never given up. I was surrounded mostly by individuals who were just marking time. I came on board fired up and ready to solve world problems, only to find out I was fighting apathy endemic to the system. My systematic learning had taught me that when you're in the middle of negativity, it's hard to see what's going on. The solution is to know better and to step out of the negative environment to change your perspective.

You have to be able to know that it's negative, number one, and then you have to know what you need to do to step out of the environment. Once you're out of the environment, the environment doesn't go away, but you can recognize it for what it is. Then you can make an action plan to try to fix the challenge you have identified in your clearer perspective that needs to be corrected. In many cases, you can't change the environment due to its permanence, so you have to change your positioning. You need a clear understanding of the system, and a situational awareness of your surroundings to know where you stand. These are fundamental Rules of the System. The most important aspect here is once you know, you have to let your instincts kick in and follow them. Never second-guess your gut. We all know when something is right and when it's wrong. You can't be afraid to make that call no matter the outcome.

What I found throughout the many challenges I've had in my life is how much people dislike change. I've learned things are predicated on your desires and willingness to achieve your outcome. Are you willing to put it all on the table to reach your goals? The internal question is about where you want to go with it, and it determines your driving motivations and your level of success.

Part of my team's responsibility was to go out and get all the scientists and experts to initiate this new level of accuracy in GPS. At the same time, we had the Gulf War beginning, and things were happening in the Middle East that required U.S. involvement. With what President Clinton did with the GPS equipment caused our Soldiers, Sailors, and Marines to be issued faulty equipment that did not meet the criteria necessary for wartime. The commercial companies developed GPS equipment that was not militarily regulated, built, or tested for the wartime environment. This problem caused military units to call airstrikes on top of themselves, which is called spoofing the GPS signal. This problem alone caused my team to spend an incredible amount of time working to resolve the issue. We had to develop a new radio that had Nav War and GPS anti-jam capabilities. Now on top of focusing on that issue, there were still office politics taking place. Once again, because of my past experiences, I was able to recognize good politics and senseless politics.

As I worked hard to focus on the issues at hand, I quickly grasped how the government workforce operated, and how I would need to perform to achieve success. As an experienced system acknowledger, the quicker you realize what's going on within the system the better positioned you are to make changes to remove yourself while working within without disruption of your surroundings. It is critical to understand where you stand while working in the challenging system in which you find yourself. You have to be savvy at all times. You need to know your support system internally and externally.

One would think government life would be very similar to military life because it's all under the umbrella of the Department of Defense. I learned there's no comparison. Government Civil Servants and Military members live in two completely different systems. The big government is bureaucratic with no accountability, and you are inundated with getting certified or forced to use difficult training systems. In most cases, this was a complete waste of time. The military is just the opposite. There is a streamlined organization where everyone is held accountable. Because these two systems are so different, you have to move about these systems with a full understanding of each, because one will not work in the other. It's extremely important to know the difference.

I tried to overlook the lazy personnel showing up to work, or the ones who never had a leadership position but stood proud on their nothingness perch. The personnel who were in sync with me and had a clue of the objective of the mission were the ones I dealt with most of the time. The folks not in sync with me I handled at a distance. This is Rule of the System # 9 applied: *Stay close to your circle, which should be extremely small (1 or 2).*

You should never get completely comfortable in how you deem situations are to be dealt with because you are in an ever-changing environment where nothing is set in stone. Self-awareness doesn't mean being a psychologist or psychiatrist for yourself, but rather staying true to your goals in life. For example, in my younger years, I was not happy with the way I was living. I was not happy with living in Philadelphia and I was not happy with living in

Georgia, so I knew I had to do something to switch my environment. I did not overanalyze what was wrong with me for rejecting those lifestyles. I was aware I felt uncomfortable with them and took action to remove myself.

Interestingly enough, as a young man when I started in life, I knew I was in no position at the time to change the actual environment I was in, but I did know what I could do to change my future. I just knew I had to keep driving in a direction I thought would help me get out of that environment. Fast forward and here I was now done with the military and in a new chapter of my life. What life has taught me over the years is that through consistent determination and drive, matched with understanding your environment, anyone can achieve the goals they set. I am not saying this course of action is easy and or will always go your way, but stay focused and you will see success.

The key to making life happen on your terms is having a good support system. For me, that meant my wife and two daughters. Early on in my career, I focused my attention on my marriage and raising my children properly. At this new stage of my life with the government, we had a foundation of family that felt secure and nurtured. I could focus on matters at hand and not have the distractors of a crumbling marriage or children who lack values. Having a supportive family life helped me navigate the government and understand the government systems I had to deal with. Rule of the System #15 remained steadfast in my life: *In marriage, effective communication is paramount*. I could give the government system all my time and energy.

Let me explain what I saw in the government system. You cannot advance in your current position or career path naturally. To advance, you have to always move to the new potential better position and not sit still. The government system does not typically allow you to promote in the same position. It is important to know what you want to do and where you want to go. You have to get out in front of the promotion, do your intelligence gathering, and set up your promotion ahead of the process. You need to not be afraid to change direction or location. You can move up the ladder but you have to get out of your comfort zone.

That may sound easier said than done because you have to compete for new work opportunities and new job assignments. Ask yourself, in whatever field you are in, are there different areas you would think are comparable, and yet if you really examine them are operating in completely different systems?

Many government employees spent a lot of time in the senseless politics arena. When you look at other things in most organizations, I would venture to say that three-quarters of the politics taking place are senseless politics. If one properly assesses their surroundings early on and learns about the various systems, everything you do will help you navigate through a senseless political environment. Seize the moment.

The times were exciting and fun as a GPS User Equipment Assistant Program Manager. I was able to bring together the U.S. Army, U.S. Air Force, Coast Guard, and the U.S. Navy to solve one common problem. Not only did I have Navy politics, I had the politics of all the other services to deal with as well. But again, because of all the past challenges, it better equipped me with dealing with the new challenges. I was able to rapidly advance in the government just because of understanding the systems and knowing what systems to involve myself with and what systems did not align within the senseless politics. My recognition of the bureaucracy enabled me to be recognized as a go-getter and an individual who gets work done. I didn't see myself as being anybody special, but to others, because I I was focused on what needed to be done, I was recommended to take on more responsibility. I was recognized throughout the GPS world as an individual who knew the business and details and understood where we had been and where we were going with the GPS technology in the world today. I traveled around the United States extensively as my team was nationwide. From March of 2001 until September 10, 2001 I logged more than 63,000 air miles flying back and forth to the Pentagon. In fact, this job almost cost me my life in one of the most devastating occurrences in U.S. history.

I was at the Pentagon on September 10 in 2001, and I left my colleagues that day to head down to Patuxent River, Maryland, where we had more meetings concerning GPS. On the morning of September 11, 2001, I was in a meeting with retired military and active duty military discussing the future challenges of employing GPS weapons or weaponized systems. That morning when the airplanes hit the World Trade Center, my world changed immediately. The day before, I was standing in the areas where the plane hit the Pentagon. Some of my colleagues were injured, but fortunately none were killed. I'll never forget that day as long as I live. My wife had to go through yet one more situation I was involved in where she had no idea whether or not I was in the middle of it or survived it. The last time we spoke, I was at the Pentagon on my trip this particular time. During this time after the attack, all airlines and all phone systems were shut down across America. For twenty-four hours, my wife had no way of communicating with me.

Because of my position in the government, after 9-11, I was able to immediately get approval to drive across the country without worrying about cost or time. I had the privilege of heading down to Georgia and picking up my brother and have him ride across the country with me. That drive across the country gave us time to reflect on what was going on in the world and how important it was to understand how fragile life can be.

After 9-11 calmed down, we were able to continue our GPS development and do the things that needed to be done for the organization and the service branches.

26 ~ The Rise to GS-15

An opportunity arose for me to lobby for promotion to GS-15 in a different work area. A GS-15 in the federal government is equivalent to a Navy Captain or a Colonel in the Army or Air Force. All of a sudden, accepting this promotion elevated me to a position where my colleagues were now Navy Captains who were Commanders of naval bases, and two-star and three-star Admirals. Working at this senior level of the government allowed me to put organizational policies in place. This level was new and exciting to me, and I truly learned a lot about the big-picture view of how things work from the big government and senior military perspective. This level of awareness will afford anyone in the system the ability to move strategically around the chess board. Again, you have to want to climb this ladder to achieve the greatness you are seeking. You cannot go after this half-heartedly. It has to be all in or nothing.

I also learned at that level how society works. I'm here to tell you our country does not operate fairly across the board. At different levels, you have changing requirements and issues to contend with all the time. Entering this new senior level of military service as a civilian, I was privy to the major differences between operational decisions and policy organization decisions. In order to understand big government operations, it takes an individual who understands the big picture and the difference between the varying levels of society. If you've never furthered your education higher than high school, you will probably struggle to understand the critical thinking required to operate at this level. This is not to put anyone down, but the reality is such that you have to be able to think deeper than what's on the surface. If you find yourself in the system at a high level and frustrated, find a mentor who has a different level of education than you to bring you through. The big picture is global society, global politics, the gross national product and so forth and so on, not the micro view we see every day.

I was moving up the ladder pretty quick as a GPS User Equipment Assistant Manager, but for me to get my GS-15, I had to leave the GPS program. I was not afraid to make the change. Working the GPS program was what we call an operational program. I had to go to the Pentagon to talk to acquisition managers about presidential funding. I had to understand how the dollars worked between military spending, civilian spending, and contractor spending. It was a very complex environment. Now I moved into the policy and guidance section of the government. Here we wrote various policies and we enacted several directives on how the government should operate. In this capacity, getting things done was very difficult. Having the ability to direct someone or an organization to do something is difficult, but if you're not responsible for the dollars that control their organizations, you have little or no say at all. This was the new job.

I took on the new job on the policy side as the Program Director for Readiness and Logistics for the entire U.S. Navy. I was also the program manager for global distance support and in-service engineering activities. These three roles were very high-level, which involved organizational departments outside of my command that I was now responsible for to other leadership in different commands. I wasn't so concerned about the new job. I was up to the challenge. I had been responsible for much larger organizations in my past, so I knew I could handle something as simple as writing policies, getting them implemented, and enforcing them. Little did I know what I was going to be up against working in this new role! I was caught off-guard thinking that senior individuals played fair. I was wrong. There was more unspoken maneuvering that transpired than I was aware of. There was collusion in the buddy system that was unbelievable. However, it was important that you knew this but could not prove it, so you had to figure out who were your allies you could trust. At this point, I was very familiar with Rule of the System #10: *Be discerning about whom you trust with your ambitions.* You always had to walk around with your eyes wide open.

In my former position as the manager in the GPS program, I had very motivated GPS people as operators. But on the new job in policy and guidance, I had a whole bunch of demotivated and lazy people. These new people on the policy side showed up to work and all they did was surf the Internet and go home. They had no interest in supporting the United States military fleet. Their whole objective was to come to work, get paid extremely well, and go home at the end of the day. They had an extreme do-nothing attitude.

Most of the daily conversations would be about "Oh, I got a new boat" or "I have a new car" or "I just went on an exotic vacation." Very rarely did you hear a conversation like, "How can I improve getting solutions to the warfighters who need them?"

I had my operational hat on when I took on the new job and I operated very aggressively. I wanted to be the new problem solver on the policy side. The second challenge was funding concerns for one organization that had been going on for several years. I was a disruptor breaking the status quo. The organization didn't want to fix the problem, they just wanted to use it as a tool to be an obstacle for getting things done. Here I come, Mr. Fixer, not knowing the rules of that game. I fixed the problem quickly and was called out for working too efficiently. This was bad for the lazy people around me.

I just came from the operational side and I knew all the right people. I knew how to solve this problem and I knew what to do to make it happen quickly. While I was on travel, this funding problem happened, but I was able to make a few phone calls to my former colleagues and resolve the problem quickly. This problem on the policy side had been an issue for at least seven to ten years. I resolved this issue within *half a day*. I was able to fix the problem in about *five hours*. When I returned to San Diego, I was called into the senior executive office and I was chewed out because I solved the problem too fast! He sat me down and told me I was acting like a mustang or like an individual who did not consider the rest of the organization. I was blown away. I didn't know what to do. I couldn't believe I had solved a long-term problem in five hours and he was telling me I did something wrong. He actually told me that in his organization, we did not solve problems, we build processes. I said to him only doing processes means nothing ever gets completed. "That's right," was his reply.

I knew then I had a bigger monkey on my back than ever before. My actions opened a closed door. When traversing through the unknown jungle (organization), my lesson was to learn the system before stalking through it. I stood firmly and quietly in Rule of the System #12: *Don't let the haters distract you from your objectives.* I was a go-getter in the policy side of the organization. The Commander and Vice Commander had my phone number on their speed dial because they knew I would get things done.

They would send orders down circumventing the senior executive and would come directly to me to solve the problems at hand. This always put me in a very awkward position because most of the time while I was out solving problems my immediate boss had no idea what I was doing. On one particular trip I was tasked to go around the United States and brief all of the area Commanders, including Commanders at Fleet Forces Command, The Regional Maintenance Center Commander, Surface Forces Commander, and several other two-star Admirals. I was in Norfolk, Virginia and I received a call from my senior executive. He asked me why I was briefing Fleet Forces Commander.

"Why are you calling me?" I asked him. "Why are you not calling the Vice Commander and asking him since he was the one that directed me to do what I'm doing?"

As you can imagine, this created an issue between my senior executive and me because I was a go-getter. The other GS-15 I worked with was an individual who achieved his position through ill-gotten gains. He was a lackey that just did whatever the senior executive told him to do. He was intimidated by my presence and was against anything positive I tried to do. That didn't shake me because again, I had overcome challenges of much greater magnitude in my past (like GITMO), so dealing with these guys was like child's play for me. Rule of the System # 4 kept me on the level and focused: *Never become pompous or arrogant. Adversity is not the enemy; stay humble.*

I was invited to attend the Navy's Senior Executive Business course in Monterey, California, which was a very prestigious event to attend. This was a three-week training course where we had all of the United States senior government and civilian personnel in attendance. We were briefed by the Chief of Naval Operations or briefed by the military budget Authority. We also had the authors of the "Dummy" series of books. We had a gentleman by the name of David Beshears who climbed Mount Everest seven times who told us he had a Chinese dignitary with him on one of his trips that he did not allow to reach the summit of Mount Everest. This was his biggest leadership challenge. His explanation of his decision was to point out to us that in leadership, sometimes you have to make decisions for the greater good not the political rationale. It was an amazing story he told us and was very inspiring.

This course was conducted by a three-star Admiral who had since retired, but I had served with his nephew early on in my career. He and I immediately hit it off very well. There was an individual from my organization attending this course as well who was completely out of his league and depth with the cadre of individuals attending this course. It was embarrassing to know he was from my command and others knew it. I did everything I could to distance myself from him while attending this course.

I learned a great deal from this course. The exposure to world affairs was remarkable. The level of information shared with us was at the presidential level. I was grateful I had the opportunity to be involved in something of this magnitude. When I returned to San Diego and they asked us for a summary of what we thought of the course, I wrote about a five-page response about how humbled I was and how proud I was to have had the opportunity to be in the midst of all these great people. This level of exposure is something I will remember for the rest of my life. They asked my colleague and he said it was somewhat boring because all he heard about was some guy climbing a mountain. I was floored when I was told of his survey response. To my point, this illustrates the level of individuals I was working with on the policy side of the government. On the operational side, you would have never heard anyone say such a ludicrous comment as this, but that's what I was working with in the new job.

What I learned about how our government civil servants work was eye-opening. I learned that because of the enormity of the system of our government, no one is held accountable. This is a very dangerous place to be when operating within the system. Because no one is held accountable, individuals can do whatever they like to disrupt your career opportunities. They can lie and provide mis-information to put you in a bad position. Walking in this environment, as long as you understand the system, then you walk lightly and always with your eyes wide open. But more importantly, have a plan "B" in place if things don't go the way you intend.

Everyone gets paid well and it's almost impossible to fire a government employee. Most government employees know that's the situation, and their performance reflects that lack of effort. I had a hard time working on the policy side because of the lazy, inept individuals I had to deal with daily. I did the best I could, given the hand I was dealt, but what I focused on were the individuals who were depending on me to get things done and I did my best to not let them down.

When I accepted the opportunity to work in the federal government in the GPS program, my wife said, "I know how you are and I know this is probably not the right place for you."

I had other ulterior motives for wanting to work in the government. I learned when I was a contractor with Company A and Company B prior to going into the government about writing proposals. Understanding what it meant to be a defense contractor and how as a defense contractor I could solve problems for the government outside of the government without all the bureaucratic red tape. The missing piece I needed to achieve while in the government was my defense acquisition workforce certifications and certification as a Contracting Officer Technical Representative. I was able to achieve my objectives. It was a tough trial I had to endure dealing with some of the individuals I dealt with, but I maintained my focus on my objective. To receive these qualifications and certifications would be a step up for the new company I wanted to start, and whether or not I should start my own business, but I knew now after all of this mess it was becoming a viable option.

After achieving my certifications, I started to think of futuristic solutions. I was certified as a level three systems engineer, a level three acquisition program manager, and a level two logistics expert. I was also certified as a Contracting Officer Technical Representative. Having these new certifications as a new business would make me unique.

I continued my efforts working on the policy side. I made some great achievements and other strides that made a difference for the warfighter. I was able to build a system that would allow for repairs to be done on ships and aircraft quickly. Before taking over this responsibility, if a service member had a problem with his equipment, it could take up to six months to get it repaired. I implemented a new process that brought it down to just twenty-four hours. That system is still in place today. I also implemented a process in the information technology field that consolidated several computer servers throughout the United States into one location, making it much simpler and streamlining the data was hosted by all the servers. When I initially recommended the server consolidation, I thought I would be publicly shot. I received so much pushback from so many people because my efforts were exposing a lot of people who had their own little fiefdoms. I was able to break rice bowls (jealously protected programs) and tear down walls. I was not your typical government employee. I went home every night satisfied with my accomplishments. Rocking the boat wasn't something most would do, but I had a plan B if it went south. One thing in the system I learned is you cannot be scared to make decisions contrary to the area you are working within.

I may have pissed off a lot of people but that was okay because what I did was for the right reasons. I did it for the warfighters, for the men and women out there on the pointy end of the spear protecting our country. I wasn't going to go into the private sector, or even this time in the government, without taking into consideration my time on the firing line with so many men and women whose lives were on the line. I served twenty-two years in the Navy and the last thing you want to have happen when you're in the heat of the battle is pull the trigger of your weapon and it doesn't fire because of faulty equipment. Or the ship doesn't stay on course and collides with something. My personal experiences ignited my passion for ensuring that when a Soldier, Sailor or Airman pulls the trigger on whatever weapon, it worked as designed. I enjoyed my time and accomplishments in the government. It strengthened the already existing beliefs I had of doing what's right for the right reasons, staying the course despite adversities, and never letting someone or something distract you from doing what's right.

I survived with great lessons and knowledge gained by dealing with others around me. The challenges I endured all had significant meanings, and I believe they were preparing me for the future. Despite all the things going on in the world, I continued to focus on the goals I had set for myself and to do what I thought was right.

27 ~ Crash and Burn into the Business World

I was starting to think more seriously about starting my own business. My wife and I had attended a seminar about doing business with the government. We had a little side business of silk screening and embroidery. It wasn't something we had put a lot of effort into; it was just something to do in our garage at home. It was a way the two of us spent time together. At the seminar, the person running the event asked me about my background. I told him what my GS status was, how I was a service-disabled veteran, and a Contracting Officer Representative. I was still in the federal government. He was very impressed with my credentials and offered me an opportunity to work with him teaching classes on the weekend to other small businesses on how to do business with the government. I accepted this opportunity and I started this work during my time off from the government. I was earning more money as a facilitator on the weekends then I was as a GS-15 for the federal government, and minus the nonsense! This opportunity went on for about two years, and the more and more I thought about it the more and more I enjoyed the freedom of working independently.

One day I went to my government job, and the guy who achieved his position unethically said something stupid to me. Before I reacted, I thought about how my initial instinct was to give him a right cross and knock him out. The fact I started thinking violently toward this guy told me immediately I needed to change my environment.

I am not a violent person and to have this strong an emotional reaction scared me.

I said to him, "Instead of getting physical with you, I am going to call you my inspiration and motivation."

He looked at me funny.

"You have inspired me to do something I have been wanting to do for a long time," I told him.

I walked away and told my wife that night I was going to leave the government and start my own business.

"In the twenty-five years we've been married I have never questioned your decisions, and I'm not about to question them now," she said to me. Having a great partner had always allowed me to take the risks necessary to go to the next level in my life, to find a new system I could apply the rules to, and excel. Even if I failed, just the act of trying to improve my life was commendable. Should you feel in your bones that the time has come to make more of yourself and expand your horizons, lean on your support systems and take the leap.

I didn't sleep that night. I was full of excitement and I could hardly wait to get to work the next day to turn in my resignation. I had no idea exactly what I was going to do but I knew what I wasn't going to continue to do, and that was to deal with the moronic environment I was in.

I turned in my resignation the very next day and it was interesting because I got my dates wrong. I thought I put in two weeks' notice when actually it was a two-day notice, so instead of correcting the problem I left in two days. A thousand pounds of pressure was lifted off my shoulders and I felt a new-found freedom when I parted ways with the federal government. I was optimistic about my leap that early July morning as I signed my standard form 50. I was ready for the next chapter ahead of me. I had a few leftover clients from my business-to-government consulting days. I reached out to a few of them and they continued my service. This provided me minimum revenue to keep the lights on in my home. It didn't dawn on me until about a week later I had made a decision for the right reasons, but I wasn't questioning if I was properly prepared for the transition. I assumed I was in a better place than I was. The work I was doing as a consultant would sustain me long enough to get my new ideas goings.

Everything now looked fine and I was off to the races. I was in perfect alignment with the trajectory of my life I had haphazardly planned. I had no idea what lurked around the corner, which was a disastrous course I would have to detour on before I could celebrate this new freedom. The company I was working for was beginning to conduct themselves somewhat unethically. They began to slow-pay me for work and would make statements that made me feel uneasy. What I didn't see coming was the next event that happened. The detour was three months after leaving the federal government, taking a severe pay cut, I discovered the group I was working for went bankrupt. Not only did they go bankrupt, but I learned that when someone files bankruptcy, the courts goes after the last unsecured debt that was paid for the past ninety days. The court system wanted me to pay back three months of payments I received amounting to roughly $50,000 dollars! There was no way on God's green earth was I going to give back money I rightfully earned to the scoundrel who was just playing the system. The owner of this company was well-versed on how the system worked and he clearly did not give a crap about me or my other colleagues.

Welcome to reality. Welcome to learning the lesson to better vet companies and only deal with trusted ones. You can become very savvy in your system and very comfortable navigating in your world, then suddenly you get launched into a different thought process. You are now dealing in an unfamiliar environment with a much smarter opponent. Once again, it's time to step up and figure out the new system, not run or give up. The lesson can be painful, but you have to go through the entire process. Accept the outcome, however the chips fall.

He filed bankruptcy one day for a company that wasn't working, and the very next day paid $1.8 million in cash for a beautiful home on a lake in Orlando, Florida!

I was somewhat upset about this, and fortunately, my friend who was the Staff Judge Advocate in the Navy while stationed in Guantanamo Bay worked for a law firm in Tampa that was well-versed in bankruptcy proceedings. As a friend he was willing to take on my case for free. This was just one of ways the long-lasting relationships I built when staying on the right side of the law and the system in the Navy would pay off for me. He said we would go through the court system and I would be able to only have to pay about $5,000 to get this guy off my case. I was so upset. "How could anyone be so heartless and so uncaring and just be so money-focused?" I asked my friend. Rule of the System # 11 is rough to embrace but it exists for a reason: *Don't take anything personally. This is a waste of your time.*

This guy had no concern for my family's well-being. I was trying to understand why someone would be so careless and unconcerned about the people who worked for him. Because of my lack of discernment and to help me understand his mindset, I called my friend John and asked him how someone could be so heartless. He gave me this analogy: Jeffrey Dahmer thought what he was doing was right. Wow, what a reality check. It helped me understand the logic he used to screw all of us who worked for him. My point in saying this is to remind you when you use the system, the system has no emotions, just actions. The lesson was you may have your perspective, but there's more to the story than just your perspective. I learned you have to be in tune enough with what's going on in the world around you and in tune with the way life really is to understand how things don't always appear to be the way you see them. There are people out there who have mastered deception. Surviving this situation meant I had to make some solid choices. One decision was to not go running back to the government for my job. I made a pact with myself and the pact was "failure is not an option." This meant if I had to work at Burger King or McDonald's then that is what I was willing to do to survive.

28 ~ PLAN B

I had not faced this kind of financial turmoil ever in my life or career. My youngest daughter was just entering college, my mortgage was over $6,000, and I had the usual car payments and other bills. I truly had to dig deep internally and I had to do a lot soul searching, praying for strength and clarity. I knew if I stayed focused and I worked hard I would make it through this situation.

What I did from this point on was truly begin to hustle. My plan B had to go into effect, which felt like "make it up as you go." Sometimes when you think you have a solid plan, nothing goes the way you want it to. But instead of getting frustrated, you have to take one step at a time in a calculated manner. Your objective should become very clear and you have to be precise in choosing your allies and enemies. Your enemies can be your greatest support if used correctly. To survive, Rule of the System #14 is helpful: *Always have rainy-day money.*

I reached out to old friends and colleagues for advice and assistance. From teaching small companies how to do business with the government I learned a lot about that process in itself. I started searching state and local government for opportunities. One of the first opportunities I received was to bid on a contract for toner cartridge for all the DMV (Department of Motor Vehicles) locations in the state of California. I won that bid, now it was time to supply the toner cartridges. Interestingly enough, the person who said they would be my supplier was unethical and I was unable to use them. So as God would have it, I was able to find a company willing to supply the products on credit based on my credit record and good reputation. The break I needed had come and my confidence was boosted. This opportunity worked out well, and even though I underbid the cost, I still made a hefty profit.

I was beginning to learn how this new system works. Learning a new level was interesting, because I had to change the way I was thinking. Not that my thinking was wrong, but it was different. I learned that in order to survive, you have to be open to change and not hold on to historical logic.

Through this contact I was introduced to a company out of Kansas City, Missouri that thought highly of me just from our first meeting. They wanted to do more copier toner business with me, and it wasn't from a lack of trying; it was just no other opportunities came forth. What they did do was remember me when they had a friend who needed a service-disabled veteran to help them with an expiring contract. They called me up to be that person. What another awesome break! This contract was for $2.6 million. This was my first real contract after being out of the government for only about twelve months. Things were starting to turn for the better. I wasn't out of the woods by far. I still had a long way to go, but I had a strong faith and I had encouragement from the past winnings.

I continued my consulting gig with companies I left. I even tried to grow that a little bit by having my daughter come in and work with me. Because of my experience and my government knowledge, most of my clients did not want to work with anyone else but me. It was no reflection on my daughter—she did a great job doing what I instructed her to do, but I learned people are very particular when it comes to spending money.

As I started progressing down this path again, there was a lot of soul-searching on the direction I should go. I thought maybe I should go back into the government, but my pride would not let that happen. I asked myself questions about why I was doing what I was doing with starting a business. I believed in myself and knew I could do it. My next question was, could I possibly succeed? I knew if I worked hard, then it would pay off. I believed and trusted God to lead me in the right direction. My other thought was how hard will the journey be? These were the internal questions I struggled with as I made this transition.

I thought about practicing what I was preaching to others. So I found who I thought was a good mentor to help me through initial rough times. The individual I was calling my mentor was a gentleman I had known for several years while I was in the government. I actually helped facilitate him being awarded a $5.5 million contract. I thought he was a good guy, initially showing himself as a devout Christian who went to church every Sunday. As a matter of fact, he was the superintendent for Sunday school and a deacon in the church, so there was no reason for me to question his character. Well, the lights in my head started coming on when I went to him for help and support and the first thing he did was somewhat demeaning.

Here I was a brand-new CEO and he looked at me as if I was a brand-new college graduate with no experience. His idea of helping me was to have me work for him at $30 an hour doing some incredibly mundane tasks. The tasks he wanted me to do were things I would not have given to an elementary school kid. I was somewhat shocked and taken aback, but I played his game to see how far he would go. I missed a very valuable lesson here. Someone told me that when someone shows you who they are, you should take a picture, because that's who they really are, and always were. My other mistake was not listening to my inner voice. I hadn't believed in the unscrupulous nature of his system, and I had challenged it to my own detriment. Yet I was still willing to give him a chance to prove himself.

Rule of the System #13 is critically important, especially when you are in a position of wanting something. You may have skewed judgement. It is always best to *cut ties quickly if someone is not aligned with your vision.* You need to focus your energy on creating the foundation to lean on to know how to cut and run. He failed at every opportunity I gave him. The next opportunity that arose was a contract out of an area I used to be responsible for when I was in the government. I knew he did a little work on this contract, so I thought teaming up with him would be a great idea. We knew all the same government players, and they knew me very well. They knew how put together the right team and it was a great opportunity for both companies. This opportunity was worth roughly $67 million. While we're putting the proposal together, we were collaborating and sharing ideas in his office. The budget proposal was nothing more than an Excel spreadsheet that incorporated our strategy on how we would price out this contract. The two of us had formed a joint venture together. I was 51% owner as the managing director and he was 49% owner as a partner. As we completed the spreadsheet, I asked him for a copy so I could go back to my office and study what we had done, simply because this was all new to me. "You know this document is my proprietary information," he said to me.

I was seeing how I did not follow Rule of the System #10: *Be discerning about whom you trust with your ambitions.* Now I was stunned and bewildered. I couldn't believe what my ears had heard. We are working together on an opportunity. I am 51% managing director and he tells me that the information was proprietary to him? To this day, I can't figure out what his mental logic pattern was concerning this effort. That was a big red flag I should have paid attention to immediately. These two incidents happened and were very significant in our newly formed relationship. Critical lesson: When someone shows you who they are, take a picture because that is their truth and they will not change. Old adages like leopards don't change their spots were written for a good reason.

I was patient with his antics, but I was thinking of our long-term relationship. I was thinking more big-picture and the fact that we had a very high win probability on this opportunity. I started paying more attention to his antics. I saw little white useless lies when asked questions, and his answers to me made no sense. I would say to myself, this was a situation that did not require a lie, so why did he lie? As things turned out, when we did win the contract, oh boy, the real devil showed himself! Everything I had seen in the past, all the flags I had noted, all the little white lies, all came to fruition. This individual turns into the most horrible person on the planet. He was greedy, controlling, lying, and those were just some of the small things he did. He recommended to me the most expensive lawyer in San Diego to assist. This lawyer was also the most inept attorney in San Diego.

My partner tried to pull all kinds of little side deals behind my back knowing I was in charge of the effort. He took me to the small business administration officer two or three times, complaining I was not fair. They told him on several occasions because I was 51% owner that he had to listen to me. And he still could not get that through his thick skull. His greed was overwhelming. More interesting, his entire staff was just like him. I cannot believe someone I held in such high regard turned out to be such a horrible individual.

On another occasion happening parallel to all this, he introduced me to one of his friends who could help me. The friend knew I was new and did not have any contract vehicles and assured me he could assist with receiving some work a former colleague wanted to give me. As it turned out, my colleague believed in his friend and we put work into the contract. His friend stole every dollar of work that was put on that contract and gave me nothing. I am a brand-new company with very little revenue and with a family that has all your standard bills and a daughter just starting college. Neither one of these gentlemen could care less about my well-being. A good rule of thumb is never think someone has your best interest at heart. They have their own issues, so don't take it personally. You have to figure out your own plays and moves while in the challenge. Rule of the System #8 is vital: *Be flexible to change but stand your ground ethically.* This was my first lesson in becoming a small business owner.

The initial guy was the one who took me to the church to which I belong today. He invited me to a men's retreat. This men's retreat was life-changing for me, so much so that I joined the church. And today I am the chairperson of that same retreat he took me to. He, on the other end, has since left the church for suspicious reasons. I am very grateful for this lesson I learned. It may seem odd with all the negativity that happened, but positive things came from this lesson. It taught me about business ownership, and it taught me a very valuable lesson about trust. This new world I was exposed to made me see I was uneducated about business. I also realized there are many systems to be aware of within the system itself, and in these circumstances I did find an extremely good, honest, decent mentor. This person is my mentor today, who I found from the mess I endured. We have to go through challenges to clearly see our past mistakes. It's good to recognize we are not the smartest people and we all could use help from time to time.

The other part of this lesson was the government revealed how corrupt it could be. After winning this contract four times and a General Accounting Office protist, the government still gave the contract to someone else! Fighting this effort went as high as the Secretary of the Navy, the chairman of the Appropriations Committee, and several congressmen. This was the time when my wife and I gained exposure to how big government works. Our takeaway was unless you grease the palms of other politicians, there's no way they're going to really help you achieve anything. This was an invaluable lesson on business ownership, personal character ethics, and many of the other traits that define who we are. The time spent back in Washington D.C. dealing with all these senior government officials was an eye-opening experience.

At one event, my wife was standing next to a New York congressman's wife when First Lady Michelle Obama called her. The wife looked at her phone and said, "I don't have time for this woman right now," and continued the conversation with my wife. We were blown away. I was in an area of total unfamiliarity. My wife and I had no idea what it was like to be exposed to such high-level politics. The one thing we learned was the way the common layperson thinks is *not* the way politicians at that level think. It's very wise to know where you belong and where you don't. We were clearly in over our heads and we knew it, therefore we were cautious as we moved around the environment. It became very clear that it was all about power and money. I believe that's okay, as long as you know the playground on which you're playing. We realized we had to abandon our ideas and walk away, even though it meant suffering a major loss. But I gained some incredible knowledge. This exposure taught me about our society and how our society operates. As the old adage says, *it is what it is.*

29 ~ BUSINESS GROWTH: THE GOOD AND THE SHOCKING

We returned to San Diego with a fresh perspective, looking at everything we had endured as water under the bridge, and we learned a lot from this episode. We did not harbor any ill feelings, nor did we stay focused on the past. We continuously looked forward to the future. Once you embrace the system, then you know that holding on to emotions is useless. It doesn't mean you can't forgive, but you must never forget the lesson and situation. Apply Rule of the System # 2: *Stay focused on the objective and continuously re-evaluate your game plan.*

This whole event lasted four years and cost me over half a million dollars of money I did not have. In all of this, I had an angel donor who worked with me, providing me with well over a quarter million dollars. So as one deal was working in one direction, another development was working in the opposite direction—a common thread in my life. I had another angel who came into my life. I didn't know this man, but he made a major impact on me, my family, and my business. This man allowed me to use his office he was paying rent on for over a year. The rent was over $6,000 per month and I didn't have to pay a penny of it. His promise to me was that he would take care of everything until I could stand on my own two feet and pay him back.

I was so blessed when shortly after that we received our first serious major contract of $4.1 million. This contract launched the company and put us on the map, but also brought about another whole new challenge. And that challenge was finding the right people who could see my vision and follow my vision. While building your system, it only makes sense to control the team around you. This is critical because you must dismiss anyone who does not see your vision or has their own agenda.

It's easy to say you have great ideas, but it's very difficult to get others to believe in your ideas. This was my huge leadership challenge. I had people working for me. I did not receive a dime but I had people working for me who were trying to rip me off at every turn. Now I would follow Rule of the System #13 and no more second-guessing my instincts. I would cut ties quickly if someone was not aligned with my vision. Amen!

I stayed true to my principles and I stayed true to my vision. We won this contract, and then another, and then another and another. and next thing I knew I had forty or fifty employees working in my company. It was amazing to see all the challenges I had been through, all the lessons I had learned, and now I was on a whole different plateau in life. To this day I harbor no ill feelings; I only harbor an appreciation for the lessons I received.

As the company grew, all these different employees brought about a whole new change in what things I had to deal with. I had a crash course on character recognition. I learned that one's character is who they are, and it runs deeper than what you see on the surface. I was maturing in business. My exposure level was increasing, and I was learning things about myself I didn't know.

Over about a three-month period, we had four different major events happen. One of my supervisors in the warehouse was drunk at work. He was reported because he was on a forklift driving and dropping containers off the fork truck tongs. I drove six hours to meet with the team the very next day and have a discussion about zero tolerance. This was a strict corporate policy I had within this company. This supervisor sat next to me, agreeing with everything.

"Sir there's absolutely no way we could tolerate this in our company," he informed me earnestly.

I could smell the alcohol coming off of him. I let the remainder of the people go and I asked him to stay behind. "The young man I was talking about is *you*," I said as he went to leave.

He looked at me. "Yes sir, but can you give me some help?"

I said, "Yes. Hand me your badge and identification."

I had security escort him to the gate and I fired him on the spot. I'm not in the business of alcoholism recovery. We are a defense contracting firm that requires personnel to have high standards, strong morals, and the ability to carry a personal security clearance. He had violated all of those requirements.

In the same area two weeks later I got a phone call that one of my employees had been locked up over the weekend. I asked about the charges. The charges were first-degree murder and elderly abuse. I almost dropped the phone in horror, thinking I had an employee who had committed murder. Receiving more information about the situation, the victim was his mother. I was speechless. It was hard for me to fathom I had an employee who would kill his mother. He and his wife allowed his mother to live in his house in a horrific environment. They found her body in mounds of feces, trash, and all sorts of nasty things. My employee and his wife were going to and from work with his mother's dead body in the house as if nothing was going on. They had no concern about a body that was decomposing in their house. Unbelievable.

After going through this situation, I thought nothing could get any worse. Then I get a call maybe two-and-a-half weeks later from the same location. One of my guys threatened the crew by saying he was going to go home and get his .44 Magnum and come back to work and "let the air out" of some people. At this point I'm thinking this location is full of complete wackos. I just could not believe what was going on.

These incidents challenged my leadership abilities to the fullest. I did everything by the book—reporting and doing everything I was supposed to do, but I had to take a closer look at this one location. The credibility of our company and the safety of the rest of the employees were being questioned. A system was operating within my own personal business system, and it was a wild cannon. I saw the fractures in the social and political systems with the enlisted men in Cuba and on the USS Shenandoah, and now here it was, front and center on my own ship. Talk about a lesson in leadership! This was the ultimate test. I had a system to clean up, and it would get worse before it got better.

What really rocked my world was one of the guys who had been on this contract for over ten years, who was married with children, but decided it would be a good idea to write a letter on a government computer to a young navy Petty Officer to tell her about the sexual fantasies he wanted to have with her. He was very descriptive. He was also stupid enough to send this email on a government computer, which was seen by the entire government staff, seniors and juniors alike. I had no choice but to fire this young man immediately on the spot. To this day I wonder what story he told his wife when he went home that day. I can only imagine he said it was the fault of someone else at work that caused him to get fired as opposed to the truth of what he did. It wasn't my place to inform his wife as to the rationale for being fired, but I would like to believe he did the right thing.

One of the other interesting things that transpired in this area had to do with our Contracting Officer Technical Representative or COR. This woman herself was different. Every time we visited with her, as a government employee and the manager of our contract, all she would do is complain about her job, her supervisor, and working conditions. She was complaining about how hard she worked and how she never received credit for it. I was on a trip to Philadelphia, Pennsylvania when I received a call from the Contracting Officer. The COR is subordinate to the Contracting Officer.

"Allen, did your company do something wrong?" he asked.

"Absolutely not. Why?"

"Have you been counseled on anything?" He was referring to a procedure that must happen before downgrading someone's marks.

"Absolutely not," I replied.

"Then why did the Contracting Officer Technical Rep downgrade your performance evaluations from exceptional to marginal?" he asked.

I told him I had no idea. The different grade levels on your performance appraisals are *unsatisfactory, marginal, good, satisfactory, outstanding,* and *exceptional.* This woman took our grades from exceptional to marginal, which is a very significant degradation in performance. Something really terrible had to happen on the job to cause any company to fall so far down in their grades. I told the Contracting Officer I would get to the bottom of it and get back to him.

When I got back to San Diego, I jumped in my car and drove six hours to meet personally with the COR. When I met her, she was just as jovial and kind and welcoming as she always had been whenever we met. There were no indications of her being angry, disappointed, or anything like that. I continue to small talk with her for a little while and then I asked her what happened to our ratings. She looked me straight in my eyes and apologized to me. Apparently, the day when she did the ratings, she was off her medication and was having a bad day. I was in shock and it would think we had either destroyed some airplanes, someone had been killed, or maybe a building was blown up or something tragic had happened. To receive a *marginal*, something major had to have happened. The answer that she was off her medication was completely unacceptable. I shared with her in a very kind way that her simple mistake could destroy my company's reputation and prevent us from ever receiving government contracts in the future. Rule of the System #8 helped: *Be flexible to change but stand your ground ethically.*

In fact, all the Rules of the System were now interwoven into the fabric of my personal and professional operations. It had taken this long, but I had finally come to be the ideal man I had seen visions of in various circumstances in my life. It was refreshing, to say the least.

She apologized, but thank goodness we had a Contracting Officer who was on the ball enough to catch her error. We were able to stop the madness before it got outside his control.

My company had now been in business for six years and changes were occurring. I hired a gentleman who was a retired Navy captain who seemed to have his act together. He was a good guy and we got along very well. I thought he was the right guy to be my number-one leader in the company. The guy before him just couldn't get it together, but I had high hopes for this guy. What I didn't realize was his leadership style was so caustic no one wanted to work for him. You must know someone's character because this could be damning to a company if not resolved quickly.

As a matter of fact, three or four people left the company because of him. One employee who had been with me since six months after I started the company, this guy ended up firing him because he felt he was incompetent. The lesson I learned was how I put faith in someone's leadership and abilities based on what I *thought* they should have as opposed to what they *truly* had, and I learned as a business owner you have to know every aspect of your business and the people who work for you. So the day came when he and I had to part ways. As professionals should do, we parted ways with no animosity and no issues. It was a pleasant departure with the promise to try and work together in the future under different circumstances. What an interesting experience that was.

30 ~ FINDING MY "A" TEAM

Timing is everything. It's now been ten years since Omni2Max has been in business. The company has gone through many changes. All the life lessons I've been learning have accumulated to this point in my life in the system. The values, the methodologies, the lessons are wonderful, and what I've learned is unmatched to what I had ever witnessed in my life. I have navigated through many systems, steadfastly following my set of rules to get to where I am today. All the rules are methodologies that intertwine, providing a fundamental baseline for success. No matter which system you are in at any given time, it boils down to right and wrong, good and bad. Intellectual astuteness is very valuable, but the ability to step outside a situation and look at it for what it is—that's far more critical to success. Rule of the System #2: *Stay focused on the objective and continuously re-evaluate your game plan.* You also have to take the time to know your thought process and how it applies to the life you are intending to have.

The journey from Philadelphia to San Diego has been an amazing experience with many stops along the way. There are many colleges out there trying to teach entrepreneurship. There are many best-selling authors who try to talk about theoretical life experiences and how to live a storybook life. There are a thousand perspectives on what to do and how to do the various challenges life offers. I remember with my first child there was the Doctor Spock book collection to give you guidance and instructions on how to raise your child. It was really amazing with our first child how we read that book religiously and followed it to a tee. For the second child, I don't think we picked up that book at all. The same analysis applies in life.

I started my life journey with one perspective in one attitude based on my cultural upbringing and based on the lessons my parents had taught me. I had planned my life to a tee. My plan was to graduate high school at the age of seventeen, join the Navy, find the woman of my dreams, marry her, and live in the house with the white picket fence, 2.3 kids, and a dog. I actually believed that's how life was really going to be. I went down a path in the beginning not to let it happen but to *make* it happen. I was rudely awakened when reality kicked in and showed me that was not the way life is. I'm glad I was open-minded enough to see and understand reality. What I've seen is how some people never allow their apertures to be opened up enough to accept differences from the way they were introduced to the world.

My purpose in writing this book is to assist readers with the most important aspect of winning and succeeding at whatever it is you want to do: Learning the ability to wear someone else's glasses. Look through their lenses to see yourself and make the necessary changes. Self-evaluation, gathering insights and knowledge, trusting yourself, and sticking with your inherent values will help you rise through all challenges in life to be a leader in whatever field you choose, whether it is as a worker in another person's company, a business owner, a government worker, or the military.

Today, my company has been in business for ten years and it was around the seven-year mark when all my learnings in leadership in and out of the military started to gel. I've gone through many hiring and firing processes with good and bad employees. I've been sued by the so-called good employees and applauded by the bad. The trials and errors of dealing with people can be nerve wracking, or you can be grateful, but all in all you have to stay on course. In the halls of my business today, I have indirect staff I call my A-Team. This is a group of amazing individuals with outstanding talent who clearly see my vision of where this company is heading. I have complete buy-in and they are contributing to the success of the company. This has been an amazing journey and I wouldn't trade it for anything in the world. And if by reading this book something touches you and helps you enhance your life, then I've done what I set out to do.

As a company, we are now ready to rock. We've gone through all the trials and tribulations, the ups and the downs, the good and the bad. Now we're ready and we're prepared to go to the next level. To achieve the next level of success personally and professionally, we are building a plan that's very realistic and achievable. My A-Team essentially found me when I needed them, and I had the maturity to select the right people.

We have won and lost contracts, our employee count has risen and fallen, and our revenue has risen and fallen as well. Most importantly, now is when the joy comes in. I've been adopted by a ninety-eight-year-old man who I affectionately call my godfather. Spending time with him and talking about my story and listening to his story is the most wonderful thing one can ever imagine. You see, ninety-eight years ago it was a very different world even as it was also the same. There were the same systems in place then as there are now. The systems were made up of the same kinds of people then as they are now. Technology has advanced quite a bit, but that's to be expected, and as our future evolves there is more technology to come. So to spend time with him, taking him for a ride in my sports car and just spending quality time with him at church and in personal settings really helps ground me and appreciate all the things I've been through in life.

My wife of thirty-five years opened my eyes to what a relationship is about and the importance of how it takes two to achieve success. We have a very good relationship because where I'm strong she's weak, and where I'm weak she's strong. We completely complement each other to the fullest. As I was going through many of my life challenges, she was always there to support my efforts, whether they were good, bad, or indifferent. As you go through life, a strong partner will open up your umbrella when there is a storm ahead. When you try to fix all your problems alone, you don't see the simple solutions a close person like a spouse can provide. It's always good to have someone to give perspective on what is critical in the situation at hand.

For more than fifty years I stayed away from the church, although I was raised as a Christian. I totally understood what Christianity was, but I didn't understand what it really meant to be a Christian. As I traveled through the roads and challenges of life, I knew I was being guided by God. There was absolutely no way I could do what I've been through without God's everlasting protection over me and my family. God granted me the wisdom and perspective needed to see things for what they were and learn how there are things you don't understand and that's okay. I learned that not everyone who says hallelujah is a Christian. There are a lot of false prophets out there, false teachers and false believers. But it's all life and it's all beautiful, as long as you can see things clearly for what they are.

I'm not perfect. I make plenty of mistakes and I will probably continue to make mistakes, but it's not about the mistakes you make, it's about how you overcome the mistakes and avoid making the same mistake twice.

As my company has matured and developed, it's ready for the next step. I love my mentor to death because he has no stake in the company or in my life but he is truly an outside counsel that provides an unbiased, untainted perspective in a very objective manner. He helps me see reality for what it is at any given moment. I've surrounded myself with like-minded individuals. I have one very special friend who turned his life around from being a hobo to become a doctor. What an incredible transition, which required herculean strength. He had an objective greater than his conditions to get into a better life. A critical piece through any system you may be navigating is humility. I've watched people go on a successful path only to forget where they began. It's not about bragging or showing off. It's all about reaching out, pulling someone up to where you're at, and sharing with them like I have shared with you.

When you accept how understanding the system is a true benefit, then it's not hard to deal with the rules. The overarching system is the fact that we are humans. Groups of humans think a certain way, and that thinking becomes the laws of that system or that subset of life. I like to always describe it as living on one side of the fence or the other. In life, you must choose what side of the fence you want to live on. On one side of the fence are rule followers. We live in nice homes, drive nice cars, and say nice things to people. We understand what it takes to live on this side of the fence. You typically do not invite people from the other side of the fence to this side of the fence. You don't do that because the other side of the fence doesn't understand and will minimize all you have worked for. For whatever reason, be it economics, level of education, or culture, people will not understand how hard you have worked to get to where you are if they have never left their first and only system. Life can be a happy place, but you have to make it so. You have to understand clearly the system you want to abide by and the system you want to live in. This decision alone will determine how beautiful your life will be. There's even a system in marriage. If you abide by the rules in the marriage, treat each other right, communicate properly, be open and honest, and be friends, I guarantee you'll have a beautiful marriage.

The obstacles never go away. The challenges just change their form and fashion. For me they went from the streets of Philly, to the unrest of the South, to the third-world environment of the Philippines, to the cowboy ethics of Guantanamo Bay. You have to be diligent and determined to not let anything stop you on your quest. As I look back at all the wonderful things that have happened in my life, they have certainly made me be the person I am today; a person that's more cautious with decisions because rushing to determinations before I seek understanding has been trouble for me. I seek understanding before casting any type of doubt or concern about a situation.

The real question is, how do you want to be remembered? I live my life in that vein. I make it a point to only be associated with certain types of people. I don't deal with people who are negative and I don't associate myself with people who aren't like-minded. Don't let the haters distract you from your objectives! I have to respect people for who they are and know that sometimes you can't change them. When you look at your big picture and purpose, you have to align with people who understand you and your vision. Take the purpose of your life very seriously during the time you have on this Earth. I serve the church with my whole heart, I serve my family with my whole heart, I serve my company with my whole heart, and everything else I do that's important to me,

I put my whole heart into it. That's why I'm careful about my selection of who I'm willing to be around or where I'm going to go. I owe it all to the Rules of the System.

Learn from the course of my life and how I navigated life as a system, and then apply the lessons to your life. While I can't guarantee you will always have a smooth ride, you will always meet your target if you remain steadfast in faith and your vision.

God bless you and may you have Fair Winds and Following Seas.

Acknowledgments

Writing a book was harder than I thought I thought it would be. I'm grateful to all who thought my story was something that should be turned into a book. My hope is that the life I have lived will inspire others to meet life's challenges head-on and never give up. I hope something I've written in these pages will touch you in a mighty and powerful way to change your life if it needs to be changed.

First, I want to give God all the praise and glory for the life He chose for me. Without God in my life, none of this would have been possible.

I could not have had the life I've written about or the ability to write this book without the loving support of my best friend and mother of my two beautiful daughters, my wife and ride-or-die partner Diane. Honey, you have always been there for me, never wavering, never complaining, just supporting our dream. You encouraged me to become an officer in the Navy, rising through and beyond the enlisted ranks. You encouraged me to take on more responsibilities in raising our family. You have always been the glue that has held everything together.

I am extremely grateful for my two Daddy's girls. Daphane, my first who set the stage at an early age to define who she was and who she was going to be. Strong-willed and determined, despite any differences of philosophy, you stood toe-to-toe with me and defended your position. That was and is so beautiful about you. Keep doing what you are doing and life will have the same great rewards for you as it has for me. Continue to defend our great nation and serve our country. Thanks for following in my footsteps. I love you, sweetheart,

Then along came Ashley, five-and-a-half years later, who made a grand entrance at birth and hasn't stopped since. I'm not sure I've ever met anyone who maximized their time in high school the way you did. Like your sister, you have always been determined to accomplish something in life. Becoming a lawyer, I'm looking forward to seeing you in the courtroom defending some poor soul who was wrongly accused. I love you, baby. Thank you for playing basketball!

To all the country folks in Georgia who inspired me to get the heck out of that environment, I thank you. You all knew farm life was not for me.

My grandmother Allen Green was a phenomenal individual. As her namesake, I am so grateful for her love, wisdom, and encouragement. She taught me what business was about and how to maneuver within the framework of the environment. She taught me about the system of life. She encouraged me not to be afraid to take on the world and succeed. Granny, you will always be right beside me. I miss you so much.

Mom, you are my rock! I can't thank you enough for your selfless giving. You put all seven of your children first despite the challenges life threw in your path. As the baby of the family, yes, you ensured I had a few perks the others didn't get to share, but I'll continue to keep that between us. I know where I get my dogged termination from. Between you and granny, how could I fail? When the matriarchal torch was passed on to you, you stood the test of time. I miss you so much. God, without question, received two beautiful Angels.

My book coach Kim O'Hara—God directed her into my life. She is and was everything required in my life to inspire me, hold me to schedules, and guide me every step of the way. Being a coach is not an easy job. It takes a special individual to have all the right mix of traits and skills. Kim has the personality, drive, commitment, and love to make writing this book fun and exciting. I could not have begun without her direction and support. For the short time Kim has been in my life, she has had an impact that is unforgettable. I may write another book just so Kim can coach me again! She is the absolute best at what she does.

I'm eternally grateful to my Sea Daddy, Albert McCoy, who saw something in me I didn't see in myself. As a snot-nosed young sailor with a major chip on my shoulder, he taught me discipline, tough love, manners, respect, and so much more that has helped me succeed in life. I truly have no idea where I'd be if he hadn't taken the time to mentor me, despite my ignorance about life.

To my long-term friends, Larry, Vince, Efram, John, Clay, Joris, and Tommie, you each ensured a period of my life was exciting and protected. Thank you all for just being true friends. I can sleep at night knowing you will always be there for me.

To my brothers and sisters, family is family and I love all of you immensely. Without you in my life, I'm not sure how I could have made it. We changed the meaning of dysfunctional to crazy love!

There have been very special people in my life, my friend who was a hobo but changed his life to become a doctor, wrote a book, and talked about angels in his life. Doc Bell, you inspired me to write this book and I thank you

There are so many out there who were angels in my life at my time of need. Thank you. If I overlooked anyone, chalk it up to my head and not my heart!

About the Author

Allen is the youngest son of seven children. Born in North Philadelphia at Temple University Hospital, the neighborhood he was raised in was not the nicest place in town. The area today is called "The Badlands," and city oversight is minimal. The opportunity to get into trouble existed each and every day living in the city, particularly in his neighborhood.

Both of Allen's parents were originally from the South and migrated north at a young age and met in North Philadelphia. His mother was born in Baxley, Georgia. She was a self-educated woman who did housework and minimum-wage jobs. She wanted better for her life, so she migrated north. Originally landing in New Britain, Connecticut, she moved her way down to Philly via Cape May, New Jersey.

Allen's father was a trash collector for the city of Philadelphia. Born in Greenville, South Carolina, he migrated north directly to Philly. Moving the family into an economically challenged environment was all he thought he could afford for his family. Despite Allen's mother pushing him to improve, he decided the streets were more important. The family was very poor but the children didn't know it. While Allen's father was not a good father, he was a good provider. The children never wanted for anything, but they also didn't want very much because they didn't know any better.

After twenty-three years of marriage, Allen's parents divorced when he was eleven years old, and his mother moved all seven of the children to the deep South to her home town of Baxley, an economically challenged small town in Georgia in 1970. The family's financial situation was still poor, only now in a different location.

At age seventeen, determined to leave the South, Allen joined the United States Navy as an enlisted sailor, working his way up through a multitude of challenges with great success. He was selected for a commissioning program and continued to excel.

As he worked his way through the challenging military ranks as an officer, assignments placed him in the Philippines during times of political unrest, as well as Guantanamo Bay during a mass exodus of Haitian and Cuban migrants. One of the ships on which Allen served was involved in a collision at sea that killed the best officer on board.

Allen couldn't have foreseen challenges like these, and many more ahead of him, but he wasn't afraid of always moving forward in life. He completed an associate degree in Electronics Technology, a bachelor's degree in Business, and a master's degree in Computer Information Systems. He accomplished all this while also working and raising his family. He married his soulmate, originally from New Britain, Connecticut and together they raised two highly successful daughters. His elder daughter followed his footsteps into a military career and joined the Navy as Construction Battalions (SEABEE) Builder, and his younger daughter pursued her life-long passion of becoming a lawyer.

After twenty-two years in the Navy, he retired and sought new adventures in the private and public sectors. His first post-military job he was as an Aerospace Engineer, working in the Global Positioning Systems directorate at Space and Naval Warfare Command in San Diego. He was later hired into the federal government where he became a very senior government civil servant at the GS-15 level.

Desiring to accomplish yet more, he launched his own federal defense contracting business. Today, his successful multi-million-dollar company has employees across several states and continues to expand rapidly as it focuses on the challenges important to national security and the defense of the USA.

A free ebook edition is available with the purchase of this book.

To claim your free ebook edition:

1. Visit MorganJamesBOGO.com
2. Sign your name CLEARLY in the space
3. Complete the form and submit a photo of the entire copyright page
4. You or your friend can download the ebook to your preferred device

Morgan James
BOGO™

A **FREE** ebook edition is available for you or a friend with the purchase of this print book.

CLEARLY SIGN YOUR NAME ABOVE

Instructions to claim your free ebook edition:
1. Visit MorganJamesBOGO.com
2. Sign your name CLEARLY in the space above
3. Complete the form and submit a photo of this entire page
4. You or your friend can download the ebook to your preferred device

Print & Digital Together Forever.

Snap a photo

Free ebook

Read anywhere